DANIEL GRAY is the author of *Homage to Caled 3pm* and *Scribbles in the Margins*. He has v on football, politics, history and travel. His screenwriting, presenting social history on television, editing *Nutmeg* Scottish football magazine – and writing across a number of national titles. He also presents the *When Saturday Comes* podcast.

ALAN MCCREDIE is the author of *100 Weeks of Scotland*, *Scotland the Dreich*, *Scotland the Braw* and *Edinburgh the Dreich*. He has collaborated with authors Daniel Gray, Val McDermid and Stephen Millar on books including *This Is Scotland*, *Snapshot*, *Tribes of Glasgow* and *Val McDermid's Scotland*. His work has appeared in national and international publications. As well as being a freelance photographer he is a lecturer in photography at Edinburgh College.

'Mon the Workers

Celebrating 125 Years
of the Scottish Trades Union Congress

DANIEL GRAY

with photography by
ALAN McCREDIE

Luath Press Limited
EDINBURGH
www.luath.co.uk

First published 2022

ISBN: 978-1-80425-033-4

The paper used in this book is recyclable.
It is made from low chlorine pulps produced in a low energy,
low emission manner from renewable forests.

The author's right to be identified as author of this book
under the Copyright, Designs and Patents Act 1988 has been asserted.

Printed and bound by
Robertson Printers, Forfar

Typeset by
Main Point Books, Edinburgh

Text © Daniel Gray/Scottish Trades Union Congress, 2022
Images © Alan McCredie/Scottish Trades Union Congress, 2022

Dedicated to trade unionists past, present and future.

Contents

Foreword by Rozanne Foyer — 13
Introduction — 17

PART I
VICTORIES

Justice for Surjit Singh Chhokar
Aamer Anwar — 25

Teachers' march for better pay
Adine Jones, Alison Beattie, Gillian Macfarlane and Leah Anderson — 32

50/50 Campaign
Agnes Tolmie — 37

Wick Wants Work
Allan Tait — 40

Free School Meals
Andrea Bradley — 43

The battle of Kenmure Street
Anonymous — 46

Apartheid, Mandela and Scotland
Brian Filling — 51

Freedom From Fear for shopworkers
Caroline Baird — 55

Fast food workers rise up
Claire Peden — 57

Opposing dockyard privatisation
Colm McConnell — 60

Call Centre Collective
Craig Anderson — 63

UCS work-in
David Cooper — 66

1985 Teachers' Strike
David Drever and May Ferries — 69

Better Than Zero
Eilis O'Keefe — 74

Pharmacists prescribe change
Gordon Finlayson and Paul Flynn — 76

Stopping NHS privatisation
Grahame Smith — 80

Responding to Piper Alpha
Jake Molloy — 83

Defeating university pension cuts in 2018
Jeanette Findlay — 86

Standing together for equal pay
Jennifer McCarey — 90

Caterpillar lock-in
John Foster — 94

Abolishing fire and rehire
John Kelly — 98

Building a winning branch
John Neil — 100

Time for Inclusive Education
Jordan Daly and Liam Stevenson — 103

Menopause policy for railway workers
Kim Gibson — 109

Bargaining for NHS workers
Lilian Macer — 112

Keeping guards on trains
Mary Jane Herbison — 115

Saving the Fife yards
Michael Sullivan — 118

From Polaris to a Scottish Parliament
Pat Milligan — 122

Saving school kitchens
Paul Arkison — 124

Saving skilled jobs in a pandemic
Paul Leckie — 127

Blind workers' rights
Robert Mooney — 129

Battle for Royal Mail
Tam Dewar — 131

Repealing Section 2A
Tracy Gilbert — 134

PART 2
WORKERS FOR CHANGE: PORTRAITS

A note on the photographs
Alan McCredie — 137

PART 3
IDEAS WORTH FIGHTING FOR

Black Workers' Committee
Anita Shelton — 173

Resistance, unity and pensions
Cat Boyd — 176

Fighting for older workers
Elinor McKenzie and Helen Biggins — 180

Women's Committee prison visit
Janet Cassidy — 186

By artists, for artists
Janie Nicoll and Lynda Graham — 188

Helping the firefighters of Palestine
Jim Malone — 191

Visiting Palestine
Liz Elkind — 194

Michael's Story and International Workers' Memorial Day
Louise Adamson — 197

Another side to the miners' strike
Margot Russell — 200

Playing the union card
Michael Devlin — 202

Learning on the job
Michelle Boyle — 205

Anti-fascism, then and now
Mike Arnott — 207

A workers' newspaper
Ron McKay — 209

Marching against racism
Satnam Ner — 212

Solidarity with Chile
Sonia Leal — 215

Union learning and growth in the taxi trade
Stevie Grant — 219

Justice for Colombia
Susan Quinn — 221

Solidarity visit to Bhopal
Tony Sneddon — 224

PART 4
THE STRUGGLE CONTINUES

Pardon for miners
Alex Bennett   229

Safe Home campaign
Caitlin Lee   232

Working together for climate justice
Catrina Randall   236

Protecting black workers in a pandemic
Charmaine Blaize   239

Climate and unions at COP26
Coll McCail   242

Worker safety during Covid
Deborah Vaile   244

Unionising produce workers
Derek Mitchell   246

A unique LGBT+ network
Eilidh Milliken   248

Changing the music industry
Iona Fyfe   250

Making a stand with Macmerry
Keetah Konstant   252

Battling labour casualisation in academia
Lena Wanggren   254

Action on Asbestos
Phyllis Craig   256

Asda equal pay
Rose Theresa Skillin   259

Carers during Covid
Shona Thomson   261

From Timex to Better Than Zero
Stella Rooney 265

Workers in the gig economy
Xabier Villares 268

Acknowledgements 270

About the STUC 271

Foreword

Rozanne Foyer, STUC General Secretary

IN APRIL 2022 the STUC held our 125th Congress in Aberdeen. It was my third Congress as General Secretary, but because of coronavirus, the first where I got to see and speak in person with the reps and activists who hold our movement together.

And as we came together again after three years apart, I could not help but think back to the STUC's Centenary Congress, held in Glasgow, in 1997. I was a young shop steward and member of the STUC's Youth Committee. I had been invited to share a platform with the legendary Scottish miners' union leader Mick McGahey to open the event. I was honoured. I was also terrified.

His brief was to talk about what our movement had achieved in the first 100 years of the STUC's existence. Mine was to look towards the struggles that lay before us. I need not have been terrified. 'We are a movement not a monument!' said McGahey. He left the audience in no doubt that our first century had been a story both of struggle and change and that the future would be no different.

This is the central inspiration for this book.

Our movement's history is rich with great victories and, also with glorious defeats. Perhaps though it is a story that has too often been told through the lens of our leaders, rather than those who won the victories and who suffered most through those defeats. Our more recent story has too often been stereotyped by commentators as one of inevitable decline. For those who don't see us or who don't want to see us, our story ended in the '80s, crushed by Thatcher and the inevitable force of the free market.

This book says otherwise. It celebrates our past, but it is also a reflection of the sheer diversity, the optimism and the energy of our contemporary movement. It tells the story of a wide range of battles fought and still being fought. It shows how often we win. It is testament to the amazing army of workplace reps, shop stewards, health and safety reps, equality reps and learning reps who are the glue that holds our movement together.

These are the true leaders of working people.

It is they who are making change in workplaces, who are organising new groups of workers and who can take their part alongside the communities of Scotland, in fighting for change.

We are still the biggest membership-based organisation in the country. Daily we support workers to fight back against exploitation. Unionised workplaces still win better pay and conditions for workers. At a time when working people need a strong force on their side, Scotland's trade unions have never been more relevant – or more necessary.

So, when the STUC General Council commissioned Daniel Gray to write this book, I could not have been more delighted. His concept of 75 stories and 50 images celebrating struggles past, present and future, and reaching across our movement, was perfect. How better to show that we are proud of our past but also focused on, and organising for, the future?

We could have chosen ten times the stories and pictures, and even then only scratched the surface of our diverse movement, our complex history and our hopes for the future. Nevertheless, the task of sourcing and collecting the stories and images that make up this book was a huge challenge in itself. Both Daniel Gray and Alan McCredie went above and beyond. But it was also in no small part due to the work of our 125 Project Advisory Group, to Deputy General Secretaries Dave Moxham and Linda Somerville and to Yusef Akgun, who has been working with us on the 125 project as a paid intern under the John Smith Centre Programme, and who did so much of the legwork for this project.

Then there are the story tellers themselves who have been so generous with their time, and with their memories. They have brought our movement to life. On more than one occasion reading their words brought tears of pride, joy and sadness to my eyes. They have made this not so much a book about the STUC as an institution, but a book about a whole movement. This is a story where the STUC is the common thread, running through the heart of the book that draws all these people and campaigns together in our quest to make

Scotland and beyond, not just a better place to work, but also a fairer place for all workers to live.

These stories have filled me with pride and optimism. They show that it is often when things have been at their worst that we have risen best to the challenge. So many of the story tellers talk about the power of the collective and for me this is the best way, the only way, to secure a better future.

So, I hope the stories in this book will help workers draw strength and inspiration from the many victories we have won – from securing the eight-hour working day to the UCS work-in; from our support for the International Brigades fighting in Spain to our role in the anti-apartheid movement; from the anti-poll tax movement that started the downfall of Thatcher to the successful campaign for a Scottish Parliament; and on so many more occasions, organised labour in Scotland has played a key role in changing the course of history and improving working class people's lives for the better.

Today we face huge challenges like delivering a real people-centred social and economic recovery from the coronavirus pandemic; delivering a just transition to a greener economy to tackle climate change; protecting innocent people from the horrors of war and imperialism; and taking on the cost-of-living crisis by ensuring that ordinary working people get a proper share of our country's wealth. These challenges demonstrate that if ever there was a historic moment for our movement to act, it is now.

The current circumstances demand that working people stand up together and start fighting back. Right now, you can feel the anger building and the collective power growing once again. It won't be easy, and we won't win every battle ahead, that's why the great McGahey also said 'they don't call it a struggle for nothing.'

But I have no doubt that through our campaigns in workplaces and communities, real progress will be made for workers in the years ahead and our greatest chapters have yet to be written. Because history shows us again and again that when we come together, our collective people power is irrepressible.

So, we will keep fighting injustices, whether new ones or those same injustices identified by those who have gone before us. I take great inspiration from our early STUC Secretary Margaret Irwin. She was a remarkable and brave woman, a Suffragist and a union organiser of women workers. She was instrumental in bringing the STUC into existence and at our first Congress in 1897, she bravely stood up in a highly male dominated environment and spoke out about the injustice of women having to do the same work for half the wages of men. It's on her shoulders that the equal pay strikers of Glasgow stood in 2018 when 8000 of them took to the streets and won life changing sums for themselves and their families, securing over £550 million in compensation for longstanding pay discrimination from their employer, the City Council.

Like so many of the stories in this book it proves that when we let a movement build, when we educate, agitate and organise, and unite to speak with one strong voice, we are more powerful than we can dare to imagine. What at first might seem impossible, can be achieved. So, remember: the workers united will never be defeated! Long live the STUC! 'Mon the Workers!

Introduction

Daniel Gray

A BLOSSOM TREE stands sentry outside the door where Margaret Irwin, founding sister of the STUC, used to live. On this grumbling spring day, the wind puffs its loose petals through the air like berserk confetti. Their flamingo pink clashes with the whale grey ground, a peace offering to the elements. 'Ach well,' says a man passing by, 'Could be worse. Could be snowing.'

Brook Street in Broughty Ferry is a long road in which pleasant homes give way to useful shops. Away from the leisure and frippery of the town's Tayside front, it is where locals are to be found. They talk on corners and tick off errands on handwritten lists. In a thousand ways it has changed since Margaret's time, and in a thousand ways not. Then again, the same could be said of the injustices this titan of the trade union movement railed against from the late Victorian era until her death in 1940. The jute mills of neighbouring Dundee may no longer hiss and clank, but inequalities hang now beneath different roofs, lingering in the call centre and the supermarket.

Margaret was born upon the waves of the China Seas, the daughter of a ship's captain. Back settled on land, she attended the private Dundee High School and then Dundee University College. These were lofty beginnings compared to, say, a mill worker's, but Margaret was never detached from the majority class around her. In fact, she had an umbilical link to their troubles, and was especially attuned to the abject conditions faced by women at work and home. She was no far-removed do-gooder, squiggling letters of disappointment to 'Sirs' or 'Whomever it may concern'; she occupied the frontline, whether protesting, plotting or traipsing the tenement stairs of Dundee or Glasgow or Greenock to talk to the afflicted.

Leading roles followed. In 1891, Margaret was made full-time organiser for the Women's Protective and Provident League, seeking to highlight the plight of female workers and encouraging them to unionise. A year later, she became Scottish Organiser of the Women's Trade Union League, and then a Lady Assistant Commissioner with the Royal Commission on Labour. Through her diligent reporting on working conditions in shops and laundries, and of the backbreaking expectations placed on housewives, she was able to scream in eloquence through a series of written reports. Margaret also launched scorching attacks on the pay gap between men and women – again, everything changes and nothing does.

In 1895, the UK-wide Trades Union Congress (TUC) expelled Trades Councils from membership. That same, year, Margaret became Secretary of the Scottish Council for Women's Trades, a role she would retain for the rest of her life. The trades councils she worked with saw a chance to reverse that TUC dismissal by creating something new. Throughout the following year, Margaret took part in meetings and manoeuvrings to plot what this body might be. Across 1896, she helped formulate the Scottish Trades Union Congress's (STUC) earliest standing orders. On March 25th 1897, Margaret arrived at Berkeley Hall in Glasgow for the founding congress of the STUC.

There were 73 delegates there over that seminal three-day gathering. Margaret represented 50 per cent of the female contingent; her importance to these happenings should not disguise the fact that this remained a sphere of Macassar oil and braces. Following the short, curtailed reign of one Andrew Ballantyne, that congress elected Margaret as Secretary to the STUC's Parliamentary Committee, forerunner to the General Council.

Her appointment did not represent the fulfilment of some vaulting personal ambition; Margaret took the job reluctantly and insisted it must only persist on an interim basis. In a telling indictment of her times, she felt having a woman and not a man at the helm 'might be somewhat prejudicial to its [the STUC's] interests.' That sentiment, though, should not be interpreted as a nullifying of her ambitions for gender equality. Margaret made the cause of votes for women the cause of the STUC, driving a suffragist motion through on the conference's final day. Women should have, said Margaret, 'a direct voice in the making of the laws which so seriously affect them, by extending the parliamentary franchise to women on the same footing as men.'

Then as now, the STUC she helped birth would be strictly independent of the TUC, and would aim to meld the interests of workers and unions across Scotland into one bold, unified cause. Harmony and co-operation between previously quarrelsome union factions would be fostered. Pursuing that theme of change and continuity, motions in Glasgow besides Margaret's votes for women pledge included those on Temperance and factory inspection, but also on industrial accident inquiries and tenancy law, concerns not unimaginable 125 years later when congress met in Aberdeen.

Three years on, Margaret resigned from the role of Secretary, just as she had promised. She continued to attended congresses as part of the Scottish Council for Women's Trades delegation. Her advocacy of female workers' causes helped create the climate in which an STUC Women's Committee could be formed, in 1926. It remains a key component of the STUC's work, now as then pushing for change and espousing the causes of women workers.

Until the vote was won for all women, Margaret continued her campaigning alongside her trade union work. Trade unionists were keenly aware of overlaps between issues – how, in this case, women's political equality could harness a degree of social liberation and workplace emancipation. Not everything was harmonious, of course; Margaret herself represented the Executive Committee of the Glasgow and West Scotland Association for Women's Suffrage in their meetings with the Women's Social and Political Union, but then resigned in disgruntlement with their electoral strategy.

From its creation, the STUC that Margaret knew so well was there through the red-hot moments of the following decades, through unity and victory, and through discord and defeat. In her lifetime, they and their affiliate unions were a stimulating, seminal presence in the 1911 Singer Strike and the Miners' version a year later, and the Govan rent strikes of 1915, when the government were compelled to limit the power of landlords. They were there through the tumult of George Square in 1919 and the General Strike seven years later. They – largely via trades councils – were there backing the International Brigades in the Spanish Civil War through a mammoth fundraising campaign.

Margaret passed away in January of 1940. She was at home, now 61 Kersland Street, Glasgow, a handsome tenement block in autumn-red sandstone. She had played an immense, immeasurable role in improving conditions for workers, and especially women. Little wonder that, three years after her death, female employees at the Rolls Royce plant in Hillingdon, Glasgow, felt emboldened enough to strike – with war raging – for equal pay.

The STUC she had been instrumental in establishing and the movement it was part of rolled on. Together, they were influential in making happen the great societal victories of the post-war period – the NHS, the nationalisation of coal mining and other infrastructure – and in the next decade of investment in industries like the Ravenscraig steelworks in Motherwell. That formidable joint force of the STUC and its affiliates campaigned on civic issues too, pushing for equality and against nuclear weapons. An internationalism that had found its voice during the war in Spain continued, fulminating against war and oppression across the world.

Then in 1971 came the Upper Clyde Shipbuilders work-in, the oldest story to feature in the pages before you.

* * *

The idea of this book was not to write a history of the STUC – so brilliantly done for its 100th anniversary in Keith Aitken's *The Bairns O' Adam* – but to collate a family of stories from living memory. They are told by those who were there and are there. Where there is history, it is people's history; individual voices reflecting on their part in wider events. Overwhelmingly, though, *'Mon the Workers* seeks to look forward and to declare how yesterday's struggles and victories can inform those of the future. It is a celebration of 125 years that fondly blows the candles of a cake and thinks about what went before, but then makes a thousand wishes and plans for the future.

Early in the summer of 2021, with the country still riven by anxiety over the horrors of Covid-19, we asked members of unions affiliated to the STUC for their stories past and present. We also encouraged them to anticipate themes and issues that future union work might encounter. There would be a focus on victories – well-known or unheralded – which stemmed from a feeling that this movement too often wallowed in glorious defeat. If we did cover those setbacks, we would do it by finding, where possible, victories within – the politicisation of women during the miners' strike, for example.

What emerged was a vast assortment of stories as the reader will see, from saving school kitchens to ending Apartheid, and from retaining train guards to building a green future for workers. They encompassed workplace improvements, societal issues and international solidarity as befits a movement of such range and clout. Through interviews, 75 trade unionists then told these stories, so that the voices of those who mattered most were captured. Reinforcing the breadth and diversity of the movement, their words are complemented with portrait photographs by Alan McCredie of a further 50 trade unionists. Together, the 125 people featured reflect who union members were and what they were striving for in the year the STUC turned 125 years old.

Mon the Workers demonstrates what the STUC and its affiliates do together now and will do next. The book's stories radiate with shared aims and a collective ethos. This is a movement that strives as one – with debate and disagreements along the way, of course – to empower the 540,000 workers it represents and win for them better conditions. As a number of the accounts contained herein reflect, it is also a movement that speaks up for those who suffer discrimination at work and in wider society. The Women's Committee that Margaret Irwin helped inspire is joined now by STUC committees for Black Workers, Disabled Workers, LGBT+ people, young people and a Pensioners' Forum. Peppered among these personal accounts too are mentions of worker education, a vital strand of membership driven by the STUC's Scottish Union Learning department. The continuing significance of local trades councils also glows bright. Strong too burns the flame of international solidarity movements.

What follows is not an all-encompassing, exhaustive account of everything that has happened in the recent life of trade unionism in Scotland. These are snapshots from those who wished to speak – or kindly agreed to do so – at this particular moment in time.

Narratives are driven by trade unionists themselves. There are full omissions or only part-mentions that may spark gasps. Absent are: protests over Linwood, the Poll Tax and Ravenscraig; actions at Timex and Lee Jeans; Blacklisting in the construction industry; the People's March for Jobs and the Living Wage campaign; recognition deals in the airline industry and pay wins for janitors, bus drivers or fire fighters… The list could go on, which tells its own tale of a vibrant, successful movement. Such omissions, though, were never without reason – perhaps the feeling that they had been covered extensively before, or represented that narrative of glorious failure or, quite simply, your author could not find anyone – despite best efforts – who could or would speak.

Nonetheless, the stories that follow are instructive, representative and frequently inspirational.

PART I

Victories

TOO OFTEN HAS this movement wallowed in glorious defeat. Our songs have been of near misses and downtrodden defiance. Yet for every setback there are a hundred gains. These words proclaim some of them and the grit and guile needed to triumph. They glow with defiance and unshakeable optimism, ingrained assets in the trade unionist.

These victories are all within living memory and stretch from the workplace to the world. Some may seem small to the outsider and may have been neglected in the news cycle and previous storytelling, but to those that won them and the people that benefited afterwards, they were colossal.

The words that follow encompass democracy, protest and equality. They howl against hate and division. They are about opposing actions and detrimental changes which maim lives in work and out of it. Some are about raising the barricades when the scene suddenly changes; others are the manoeuvres of long-standing, persevering campaigns. All are about standing or sitting or marching together to protect what is right or oppose what is wrong and build something greater. Here, even the seemingly tiniest of changes embody that much.

Our stories come from the expected, bold heartlands of trade unionism – dockyards, factories, mines – but also its modern hives – supermarkets, call centres, offices. Here are the yarns of fitters, fast food workers, internationalists, cinema ushers, carpenters, lawyers, lecturers, democrats, train guards, teachers, protestors, oil workers, cleaners, postmen and women, campaigners, shipbuilders and all the rest. Each of them believed this much: if people act together, they can build a better tomorrow.

Justice for Surjit Singh Chhokar

Aamer Anwar

Lawyer Aamer grew up in Liverpool, the son of a bus driver. He moved to Glasgow in the late 1980s to attend university. In 1998, a North Lanarkshire man named Surjit Singh Chhokar was murdered in a racist attack. For the next 18 years, Aamer, Surjit's family and the trade union movement fought tenaciously to bring his killers to justice.

MY FIRST INVOLVEMENT with trade unions was round about 1989 when I was becoming involved with student politics. Before the official St Andrew's March was launched, we would march around that time of year and we'd be at Nelson Mandela Place and the National Front or the BNP would turn up. There were running battles. Trade unions were always present. I would see the banners.

In November 1991, I had my teeth smashed in by the police in a racist attack. When I was crying and terrified I asked them why they had done that and they said: 'This is what happens to black boys with big mouths.' Various left-wing groups told me to go to the Fire Brigades Union (FBU) to seek support. I went to them, they gave me a helping hand, they helped me get leaflets photocopied about the racist attack. They opened their doors to me and that was the first real involvement I had. Before they knew it me and others were printing thousands of leaflets and breaking their photocopier! That became a deep-rooted friendship that has lasted many years. They taught me the meaning of solidarity. Whenever there were demonstrations, it started off with the FBU, and then the STUC, that came hand-in-hand.

Then I became Scottish Organiser for the Anti-Nazi League. That established a link with the STUC and various other unions coming on board. There was that slogan: 'Injury to one is injury to all.' I immersed myself in these ideas and that slogan came to the front, because every time something happened, I was told 'Go to the STUC, go to the FBU, they will always help you.' I was a pain in the neck and would be constantly knocking on their doors demanding support. Then, their unconditional support would come. I would speak to the Asian community and they would say, 'Why are they interested? They are white.' And I could say it was because of solidarity, and that they knew an injury to one was an injury to all, and they carried that out in practice. I saw that in practice on the streets.

In 1995, the unions were still supporting me in my own case, and I became the only person of colour in Scotland to ever win a case against the police for a racist attack. In those years, I had something like five court hearings, I was arrested 25 times, I was victimised. There were times when I was to blame, on demonstrations, and there were other times when the police would literally come into the crowd and grab me. Then there'd be a riot because demonstrators knew I'd been targeted and would kick off. Since the attack, the police had always wanted me out of Glasgow.

After that verdict, I decided to go back to university and do my law degree. In 1999, a year after the murder of Surjit Singh Chhokar, I was in my final year of doing a law degree and the Stephen Lawrence case had come out. Jack Straw had stood up in parliament and said that the police was institutionally racist. That was quite a moment.

A week later, I got a phone call from some friends asking me if I had seen what had happened in the Surjit murder case. Three white men had been named as being responsible but only one had gone to court, Ronnie Coulter, and then been found guilty only of assault. That left me despondent. I felt I needed to meet with the Chhokar family.

I went to the Sikh temple at St Andrew's Drive. I was waiting outside, I'd put a suit on to try and look smart and look like a lawyer, even though I was a final year law student. I met Manjit, Surjit's sister, and she was not hostile but suspicious when I introduced myself and said I really need to speak to her and her family. I just wanted five minutes to say that I wanted to help. I learned from Manjit that their parents were destroyed by what had happened. It almost felt like that would be the end of it.

I phoned Bill Speirs from the STUC that day. I spoke to him and I also contacted the FBU. I said, 'I need help.' I spoke to Roz Foyer and Dave Moxham too, and all three at the STUC offered unconditional support. I asked the FBU for an office to run the campaign from.

I went to meet Mr and Mrs Chhokar and I told them we were going to do a press conference, and we already had a place to do that, which was the STUC headquarters on Woodlands Road. I spoke to Imran Khan, lawyer for Stephen Lawrence's family, who has guided me a lot through my career, and he said Neville Lawrence – Stephen's father – would come up for that. He would speak, the FBU would speak, and the STUC. Mr and Mrs Chhokar were still suspicious and I remember them saying to me, 'Why are the STUC helping? Who are they?' I said that they could be relied on for unconditional support and that they would mobilise in their thousands for us. Mrs Chhokar said to me, 'How long will this take, son?' The first mistake I made in that campaign was to say, 'I suspect six months to a year.' I never in my wildest imagination thought it would take just two weeks shy of 18 years for Surjit's murder to finally get justice.

We held that press conference and all the press were there – very quickly they had called Surjit 'Scotland's Stephen Lawrence.' We knew that at that time the police didn't want to tell anyone about Surjit; they didn't want anybody to know there had been a race attack. Within days of the murder, the family had been told that two of the guys had been released and were on the streets boasting about having killed a 'Paki and got away with it.' News came through also that Ronnie Coulter had got a tattoo of Devil's Advocate on his back, which of course is a film about a lawyer who gets off guilty men.

The campaign developed huge momentum very quickly. That was March 1999, and by the summer we were having marches, demonstrations, huge public meetings. The STUC were central to that, along with the FBU, Unison, EIS, PCS, CWU and so many unions. It was very emotional. I remember many times when I'd be in tears with the family because it was a heart-breaking campaign. Mr Chhokar became seriously ill. At times the family felt they had no more tears left to shed. We just had to keep going with the campaign, fighting the criminal justice system and galvanising the campaign beyond the media and to the streets and the community. We wanted everybody to know what had happened. We realised now we were in this for the long haul.

In 1999, the family and I spoke at the May Day march. We got to Glasgow Green and I remember running into Andrew Coulter and David Montgomery, who were the other two individuals accused of the murder. They saw us and froze, and I froze. I was with Mr and Mrs Chhokar. All sorts of thoughts went through my head as I was surrounded by trade unionists. They walked very fast out of Glasgow Green.

That was the first big demonstration and rally. The support was over-whelming and moving. When we'd speak from the platform, our voices would falter and there'd be tears. My voice still falters when I think about those moments, because it was heart-breaking and it was destructive. But at every moment, the trade union movement carried us on their shoulders and gave us hope and inspiration. They kept their doors open to us. That allowed the campaign to continue through times when we faltered and argued and thought that was the end. Eventually, it felt like the whole trade union movement was on board.

In November 2000, a second trial took place at Glasgow High Court, this time for Andrew Coulter and David Montgomery. The two individuals came to court and turned around and blamed Ronnie Coulter. They said he'd boasted to his sister about killing Surjit. I remember looking round the court, and there were lots of supporters from the trade unions there wearing their orange flowers, something the judge decided was trying to interfere with the jury and they were warned. The court room was packed. The family was angry, I was angry.

In court, we'd walk across the corridor and the accused would be walking past with smiles on their faces. The family kept their dignity on every occasion. They were found not guilty and that was devastating. When the trial finished I remember holding Mr and Mrs Chhokar's hands and we hung our heads and cried our hearts out. I felt I'd let them down. I'd promised them justice.

The St Andrew's Day March in 2000 was a big moment in that, with thousands there and Mr and Mrs Chhokar leading. I think now it was the biggest anti-racist movement this country has ever seen. We had the support of every trade union organisation and branch, we spoke at hundreds of meetings across the country. The unions gave us the support which allowed that to happen.

We then called for a Public Inquiry. We had the whole trade union movement and every political party on our side, but we were being stitched up. They'd already carved it up and said there would be a Judicial, not Public, Inquiry, which was not what we wanted and was a slap in the face. We were suspicious and for months kept arguing against the inquiries because we knew they would be a whitewash, unless it was a public inquiry. We went to the Scottish Parliament the next day and the politicians praised the Chhokars' dignity and all those other adjectives that are used every time a black family is subjected to this. They didn't realise that behind closed doors, this family was full of abject rage and anger. We were heartbroken. We cried and the trade union movement cried with us.

We fought for the next six months before we boycotted the subsequent Judicial Inquiry into racism. They wouldn't do a Public Inquiry. I remember at the time saying 'Can you imagine having a Stephen Lawrence Inquiry where the family of the victim and their lawyers were not allowed to ask questions of witnesses, and where they were not given disclosure of evidence? And where it would be those responsible for the institutional racism practically investigating themselves?' We walked out. The trade union movement walked out. Every black organisation refused to cooperate. We saw it as a whitewash and when it came out a year later, it was.

By then, Mr Chhokar had developed cancer, and though the trade union movement door was constantly open, we started to wind down the campaign. The family's hearts were broken and we thought that was the end of it. After a second trial, we knew that those men could never ever be prosecuted again, and that was the end of the matter.

Years passed and we started to move on. I was a lawyer, my offices had moved out of the FBU by then! I kept on speaking at union meetings and anti-racist marches over the years. Then, fast forward a few years and the changes to the double jeopardy laws in England and Wales. Imran Khan phoned me and said, 'This is happening and we're going after Stephen's killers. You need to move for that in Scotland.' I tentatively went to the Chhokars, who by now treated me like family. Mr Chhokar was seriously ill but kept fighting back. They were both warriors.

Time had moved on, we kept up our close relationship with the STUC, and Bill Speirs had sadly passed away. We had approached the Scottish Government and they agreed to change the law on double jeopardy and then I went back to Manjit, and I explained the law had changed, and she said: 'Let's go for it. We need to convince my Mum and Dad.' So we went to see them. Mr Chhokar was very, very ill by then. We were trying to convince them to give me another chance. They said no, and that they didn't have the strength or the energy to go on more marches and to more meetings. I said they didn't have to do anything, that we would do it. I was able to say that this time I knew people who would support this – individuals in the police who desperately wanted a result, high up legal people too, including Solicitor General Lesley Thompson QC who later because of the campaign fought became a friend to the family and myself. They eventually said yes. Mr Chhokar said, 'You need to make me one promise, son: that you will get me justice this time.' I thought about it, and this was the only time in my legal career I said this, I said: 'I promise you.' Part of me was tearing apart inside, because I knew how ill he was, and I knew if this failed it could break him. He gave me his trust, and his trust to the trade unions again.

It took two or three years, but finally the High Court said that one of the three individuals, Ronnie Coulter, could be retried because of the presence of new evidence. By 2015, sadly Mr Chhokar was severely ill. He passed away a few weeks after that decision. I was one of the coffin bearers at his funeral and gave the euology. When I looked down I could see trade union leaders, but also the Lord Advocate, Solicitor General, the Justice Minister, the Deputy Chief Constable, police escort riders. That was something you could never have considered in 1998. That respect was testimony to the perseverance and the struggle fought by Mr and Mrs Chhokar.

A year later, we went back to Glasgow High Court. Things ran like clock-work. The family was treated with respect, their supporters from the union movement were there every day with their banners outside. Trade unionists who had been there throughout were all there. There are far too many to mention, but they included the likes of Professor Phil Taylor, Roz Foyer, Simon McFarlane, Dave Moxham, Lynn Henderson, Mary Senior and so many more. The trial lasted two weeks. It felt like part of my heart was gone, by not having Mr Chhokar by my side. Ronnie Coulter sat 10 metres away in the dock. He no longer had the arrogant swagger he had once, although his lawyer, Donald Findlay QC, was still the same. This was our court. It belonged to the family. They weren't victims now, they were warriors, and they had dragged Ronnie Coulter to court kicking and screaming 18 years after the murder. The word came through: Guilty.

We broke down. Mrs Chhokar turned around and said to me in Punjabi: 'Finally, this man knows how as a mother I have felt, but my husband and my son will now be at peace.' And we just hugged each other and cried.

We went back into a meeting room and hugged and smiled and cried. The young children had grown up. We pulled ourselves together and went out to the steps and made a speech. We paid tribute to the family, the Crown Office and to the police for having left no stone unturned this time. They were desperate to get justice – this was a stain on the criminal justice system in Scotland. But it wasn't a celebration, it was a relief, and the chapter was closed.

Without the STUC and the trade unions, we couldn't have got justice. We couldn't have galvanised people; we didn't have the funds and resources. We wouldn't have had the people on the streets terrifying an institutionally racist and corrupt criminal justice system and police service. Now, when cases like this happen as has happened with Sheku Bayoh, I always say to families, 'We'll go to the STUC, we'll go to the trade union movement.'

This was a textbook example of the trade union movement at its very best. Unconditional support and solidarity for a family that weren't rich, weren't powerful but had the stubborn love of a mother and father for a child, who refused to be silenced and patronised. And behind them, they had thousands and thousands of people from the trade union movement. They gave the Chhokars the feeling of 'united we stand, divided we fall – we will not be defeated'. I will never forget the debt that is owed to the STUC and the trade union movement in Scotland for what they did. They gave hope, and justice.

Teachers' march for better pay

Adine Jones, Alison Beattie, Gillian Macfarlane and Leah Anderson

Adine, Alison, Gillian and Leah are teachers at Thorntree Primary in Glasgow. Alison is the union rep and Adine, Gillian and Leah are active members in a lively union branch. After a number of internal victories on school policies, in 2018 they mobilised for the national campaign to win a 10 per cent pay rise for teachers.

Alison: When I started, I realised that there was no rep at our school. Then one day an email came from the Educational Institute of Scotland (EIS) pointing this out. I asked my headteacher if I could fill the role, she said 'yes', and that was seven years ago.

Adine: I had never been into any type of politics or trade unionism because, growing up in South Africa, everything was so corrupt that I had no interest at all. During my probation year we never had a rep in my school. I moved to Thorntree and Alison is an amazing rep who introduced me to the union world! We have a Working Time Agreement (WTA) here and that's been a huge change for me and my work/life balance. That was the first thing that demonstrated to me the importance of having a strong union branch.

Gillian: I worked in hospitality before I became a teacher and I really hadn't anything to do with unions. It was almost frowned upon in that sector. Coming to Thorntree and getting more involved through Alison, that was when I realised how important unions were. I feel like we've made quite a lot of different small changes, collectively as a branch.

Leah: I didn't know much about unions at all. I joined in my probation year. I've learned what trade unionism really means as

I've gone along, and what it can do for people, through reading and listening at meetings, then seeing the good the branch does in our school and knowing there's someone there to turn to if I needed help or have questions. It helped with my working relationship with management – having positive conversations where we all know where we stand, where the boundaries are, what my rights are, what I can ask for, where I'm looking to go with it.

Alison: Now the running of the branch is streamlined, but it took a while to get there. Because there had not been a rep for a while, a lot of my time was spent asking teachers questions – how do you *actually* feel about having to do a club after school when you don't really have the time to do that? If you are unhappy, it is something we can decide to change. A lot of time was spent telling colleagues that it's OK to challenge things.

Adine: You can't expect change if you're not active in your union. To make change you need to be active.

Alison: It was also about saying, 'You can moan about things you don't like, but here's the route to making change, and you need to be ready to follow it.'

Gillian: Membership is about knowing where you stand and knowing someone has got your back if they are needed.

Leah: Understanding that it's OK to have a work–life balance is something being in the union helped me with. Things that have been put in place like the WTA have been so useful. I never knew there was anything I could do about things like pay offers until we went for it as a branch. It amazed me, the impact a union can have when everybody works as a collective.

Alison: For the pay campaign in 2018 we spent a lot of time telling people: you *are* worth this. From a rep's point of view, it took a while to convince people that it was worth fighting for a better pay deal. There was a feeling that teachers already got paid quite well compared to some other public sector colleagues. We had to convince people that they were allowed to ask for more money, that they were allowed to ask and fight for this. They didn't just have to accept a pay increase each year of nothing or 0.5 per cent, because that wasn't reflective of their experience, and it wasn't going to help them pay their bills. It was a cut in real terms.

Adine: I knew my worth and I knew my colleagues' worth and that was what was important to me. We did have to take the public route, and our salaries are published, so we were dragged through the mud – *Teachers? You get half a year off on holidays… You're glorified babysitters… You don't deserve more money, other public service workers deserve it more* – these were some of the comments online. It was the public who seemed against us as well, so it was about getting over those hurdles, and realising that not everyone felt the same way and that we were worth our claim.

Alison: We were all still going up the pay scale, so we knew for the next few years we were going to have increasing salaries, but what I was thinking about was trying to convince those colleagues who had been earning the same amount for five or six years, while at the same time their bills and the cost of living was going up. That took a long time, persuading them that they deserved it and were allowed to ask for it. There was also the point that probation teachers should have been starting on a better salary, in line with other professional starting salaries.

Leah: I liked that it opened up a conversation about our profession. First of all there was a narrative of 'You went into this job knowing what your salary would be, it's public knowledge, so just put up with it.' The demands on us have increased year on year, the things we're expected to do and fit in. We are worth the pay increase.

Alison: The hardest part was there was a lot of discussion on 'What about other public sector workers?' and so on. We had to say that we were not taking away from anyone else's right to ask for a pay rise, and that we would support them 100 per cent, but we can't fight that fight for all public sector workers, we can only do it for us. There was negativity, but you have to not get bogged down in that discussion.

In October 2018, a huge march of teachers through Glasgow was announced. I wanted to put some information out on parents' night, but I didn't know if I was allowed. I asked the headteacher if I could put badges and posters out, she asked her boss, and it was OK. We left the table there, nobody was preaching at anybody, and a few kids came in the next day wearing the badges, which was a special thing.

The week before the march, we spent a night at school making all the placards and banners to take with us. People from other schools popped in, we took stuff to other schools along the road. We had our yellow t-shirts, which all the teachers were marching in. That night geed us all up. We had talked in theory before, and now we were ready.

Adine: The march was my first positive experience because in South Africa it used to go the opposite way if people wanted something. Things were destroyed, it was more about rioting. Here was a peaceful march where people were singing and there was just an incredible atmosphere. It was a magical day.

Alison: I think there were 30,000 teachers on the demo, dressed in yellow. I remember that feeling when we were marching – 'There's still people at Kelvingrove, and we're nearly in the town'; that ripple of excitement that we're at George Square and there's still people miles back down the road. I remember that feeling of how big it was, and that it was surely going to be on the news now, and that it was going to be a big deal. It felt like we'd won already, even though it'd not been decided – how could they not give us our pay rise!

Leah: I was bowled over by the march through Glasgow. You hear about the expected number and I had a picture in my head that was under-exaggerated a little bit. I don't think anybody predicted there would be as many there as there were.

Alison: It was a lot of people's first experience of that kind of thing. You could feel that nervousness and excitement of 'We've shut the streets in Glasgow to do this.' The power of it felt massive. You could see banners from Orkney, Dundee, so many places, and you realised how far people had come for this. The scale of it was more than anyone could've thought. How could they say no to us after that? They tried still, though! Feeling part of that collective effort was incredible. There were a couple of times I just looked around and saw the scale of it all, and thought about how everybody was there for the same reason, all freezing their toes off for the cause.

Gillian: One of the things I remember is going through the West End. You would think everyone who was stuck in a car because we were blocking all the roads would be raging at us, but they were all supporting us, beeping their horns positively and cheering us on, singing and shouting. Then we got to the bottom of St Vincent Street and looked up and you could just see this sea of yellow for miles, and all the placards. It was just crazy.

Alison: A few months later we were balloting for strike action. I had planned a yellow envelope party where we were all going to fill in our ballot papers. But we won before we even filled in the ballots, so I turned it into a victory party. We won a rise of 13.5 per cent.

Adine: We'd set out to do something, and we'd accomplished it. That was a good feeling.

Leah: I was really proud of being a part of it, having been as actively involved as much as we were. I am pleased we had those conversations with parents, colleagues and the people in our lives. I am glad I did it and I will be ready next time. We will just keep going. Now we know that it can be done, we can do it again.

50/50 Campaign

Agnes Tolmie

In 1997, Royal Bank of Scotland worker Agnes was Chair of the STUC Women's Committee. Their '50/50' campaign demanded equal representation for women in the new Scottish Parliament.

I'VE BEEN A trade unionist ever since I was a youngster. My grandfather was a trade union man, my father still is and he's 95. He was a shop steward in Singer's at Clydebank. So it was a natural part of our upbringing to be part of the trade union movement.

The battle for equal representation for women began before the campaign for the Scottish Parliament itself took off. It kicked off in the trade union movement itself. The STUC Women's Committee took on the challenge of trying to change how the General Council of the STUC was made up – it was predominantly men on there. We had a debate: where were all the women? How could they discuss equal pay, maternity rights and so on in the absence of women? If you're not at the table, you're on the menu. So we took on that challenge.

There were fabulous women around me on the Women's Committee. They were full of energy and commitment but were fed up of hearing the same arguments. It was a hellish battle to change the minds and attitudes of the men in our movement. We had the same arguments when we tried to get women selected to stand for councils or as MPs. The main argument against us was: Where are you going to find the quality? But I mean, have you met some of those men? They didn't set a high bar! We took that on. We had to stand up at congresses and say: 'We make up 50 per cent of the population, but we're posted missing everywhere.' It was hostile; it didn't happen overnight.

There was this sense building that something had to change and the Women's Committee came up with the 50/50 idea. One of the women wrote a song: '50/50 easy peasey, half for him and half for measy!' We sung that everywhere we went.

One of the key things was to win around individual unions, so women put motions forward on equal representation, and won those. That was one of the hardest things we did – changing minds and old-fashioned ideas that somehow women weren't capable, competent or clever enough. Because the Trade Union movement itself was run by and for men. Having said that, Bill Speirs, who was STUC General Secretary at the time, was fantastic. He helped really drive it. I made him an honorary woman later.

We made our 50/50 badges and sold them to fundraise. We had petitions, and great speakers from within the movement. We went wherever we were sent to speak – the last miners' gala in the Meadows in Edinburgh, that kind of thing. I made the fatal mistake of trying to keep up with Mick McGahey's whisky drinking and had to be taken home!

Education was important because a lot of *women* didn't believe what we could do. So we had these education courses run by the STUC – about public speaking, about understanding the jargon that's used in the movement. All of these different things that would build confidence in ourselves that we could succeed.

We would sit and chat and take to platforms, and when you produced women who were capable, the public went along with it and that groundswell of opinion began to change.

Once we'd won the argument that women had to be seen in the movement, the next stage was to take on the coalition for the Scottish Parliament and put our argument there. Remember, even then, there were 72 Labour MPs and only one was a woman, Maria Fyfe. That looked ridiculous. She was a fantastic ally in these campaigns for 50/50 and women's rights.

The thing for us was to deliver not just the Parliament, but the representation of women within that Parliament at the same time. Lots of women signed a document demanding the 50/50 representation for the new Parliament. I am so proud of what we did as a movement and as a women's movement, and how we came together.

In the first Scottish Parliament election, we got 40 per cent women elected in the Labour Party. The SNP embraced it too, including in their cabinets.

There is still work to do, but it's now unacceptable for anyone to try and reverse these gains. I think we have proved ourselves in the Scottish Parliament. We've had many women MSPs, we've had women party leaders, we've had policies that I don't believe we would have had if there hadn't been women in that Parliament. We wouldn't have had funding for Rape Crisis and violence against women legislation. We wouldn't have had free primary school meals.

There were battles for women all the time, and there are now. There are still a lot of fights to be had.

Wick Wants Work

Allan Tait

Allan began work at the Wick tax office in 1982. Twenty-five years later when it was threatened with closure, he and trade union colleagues were successful in their campaign to keep it open. This small band continued to defy these government plans for another decade.

IN 2009, IT quickly became apparent that the UK government were looking to combine and centralise their HMRC and Inland Revenue offices. Wick's tax office, with the town being at the top of Scotland and a complete outpost, was always high on the hitlist. We were over 100 miles from the nearest office, we were completely out on our own. It was thought: 'Well that's that, Wick will close.'

But we were quick to point out that we covered Orkney, Shetland, Caithness and Sutherland – an area bigger than Belgium. We provided a service that we felt should continue. So we were up for making the arguments to suggest that we should be still involved in providing that service. We got involved quite quickly, and it then moved from one battle to the next.

What we wanted was for the office to remain open and the jobs to stay in Wick. Our campaign pointed out local economic factors. Back then, Dounreay nuclear power station employed 2,000 to 3,000 people, and when you think Caithness has only got a population of 24,000, you can see how important that was. It was decommissioning, so that was a massive concern for employment in the future. Where were those people going to find work? That was a worry.

And, of course, we were concerned to hold onto our own jobs, relatively well paid for a rural area. When I'd joined in 1982, there were 100 people employed in that government complex in Wick, and that would've been mainly full-time jobs. Over the years they were diminished. We also highlighted that there were areas of deprivation in the county.

At the start, we got together in the office to run the campaign. I was quite happy to lead on letter writing and contacting people, but everybody took a turn. It was a major letter writing and meeting campaign to make people aware of the economics we were faced with up here, and how important the jobs were. Anybody that we could find, we contacted. We kept it high profile.

We had a good slogan in 'Wick Wants Work', and we had our Wick Wants Work metal badges and a banner that went everywhere. The union would have a conference every year, so the Wick Wants Work banner would travel all over. It went as far as Brighton. It was about building a campaign and making sure we were never off the radar. We emphasised how remote and unique we were – it is four hours by train to the nearest city, Inverness – and I think we did that quite successfully.

Lots of things came into play – not just banners, not just letters, not just lobbying MPs – it was a mixture of everything. Then in July 2011, it was announced we'd be staying open, for now at least. 'Wick Won Work!' said the Public and Commercial Services Union (PCS) press release.

The closure threats kept coming but we kept them at bay for a number of years when lots of other HMRC and Inland Revenue small offices were closed. We kept up the pressure and kept embarrassing them into keeping us open. We kept putting closure off, even if it was possibly inevitable. We did various things; for example, one of HMRC's arguments was around the cost of accommodation so we brokered a deal with the council for cheap office space again to put pressure on HMRC.

We got good support from the local community and from local agencies. They all could see the arguments we were making about employment. The person in the street could see it. They were fed up of things closing and jobs leaving the town never to return. Through that we had the support of the public, even if we were a tax office! They wrote to their politicians and to HMRC. They were very aware of Wick. And of course we had great support from the STUC.

Towards the end we were ahead of our time, as we began

homeworking in 2014. That got us another two years probably. It put the Wick issue into the long grass as they didn't have to pay for an office.

Eventually they were able to cut us off. But that was six or eight years after other offices had closed. We'd managed to keep the office open so that most of the staff had paid off their mortgages, got their kids through university… so it was getting to a stage where people could move on. Ten years earlier it was a major worry. We got beyond that stage and I think near enough everybody has got something they're happy with now. It worked out well for everybody.

Free School Meals

Andrea Bradley

The STUC Women's Committee campaigns on many issues, and the provision of free school meals has been central to their work in recent years. Here Andrea, a member of the committee and the Educational Institute of Scotland (EIS) union, explains why.

UNIVERSAL PROVISION OF free school meals has been an objective of the STUC and the STUC Women's Committee for some time. It's also a policy objective of my union, the EIS. We understand the connection between young people being fed at school and feeling emotionally secure and the relationship between those two things and their ability to learn. It also relates to wider poverty – it is one way you can take pressure off families who are relying on meagre incomes.

New life was breathed into the campaign at the 2019 STUC Women's Conference, when the focus was child poverty. Two motions called for this provision, including breakfast, and on 365 days a year, across all Local Authorities. So the STUC Women's Committee campaign stepped up at that point.

Universal free school meal provision is a tangible policy we can work towards achieving. There had already been concessions from the Scottish Government – in 2015, they began providing free school meals for all P1s to P3s. We thought we should build on that success to argue the case for all school children to get this provision. In the latter stages of 2020, we began campaigning for that. By early 2022, that provision had been extended to P5. There is still patchy provision during holidays, though. We want to end holiday hunger too.

Our view is that no child should be going hungry in the 21st century. And we know that the learning of a young person is negatively impacted if they are not getting something to eat. This also contributes to the poverty and attainment gap and affects their experience of education.

Free school meals for older children are means tested. That means that some families don't qualify but are still struggling. They just miss the threshold. Some parents go without food so their children can eat. That is wholly unacceptable. We also know that some families that are entitled aren't taking up their entitlement – that could be because of the bureaucracy involved, and there could be literacy barriers too.

We know that some older children who do qualify for free school meals suffer from an associated stigma, sometimes because of the spending limits and sometimes because some young people who don't qualify for free school meals prefer to go to the shops and buy lunch. Then it becomes obvious which kids are accessing the free meal entitlement because they're staying in school and going to the canteen, whereas the cool thing to do if you have the money is go down to the high street and go to Subway or the other takeaways or supermarkets. Those who can't afford to do that experience the stigma. Or, in many cases they don't stay in school for their lunch, they go to the shops and they don't buy anything or they buy very little, often pretending they're not hungry. I've seen children refuse to take a free packed lunch because of the stigma attached, and then going without food. They prefer to feel hungry than feel ashamed.

Universal provision takes away the difficulties that families have accessing their entitlements. It helps those that are just falling short of qualifying for provision but struggling, and it removes the stigma, humiliation and embarrassment around taking free school meals. Alongside that, it encourages people to eat a nutritious meal, together. So it creates a social experience.

Alongside other organisations, so far the STUC Women's Committee campaign has achieved a lot. It has persuaded the Scottish Government that this is the way to go, as we saw when provision to P1s and above began in 2015. We have convinced all political parties of the value of this policy, and the Scottish Government is committed to providing free meals for all primary school aged children by August 2022. That's quite something after only a couple of years of campaigning. They also committed to the provision of free meals in nurseries too. They are wins.

What jars, though, is that we don't see these arguments as exclusive to children aged 3 to 12. It doesn't make sense to exclude secondary-aged children from that offer, especially as they are the ones most likely to suffer stigma and shame if they qualify for free meals. Hunger knows no age boundaries, and that's why we're continuing to push.

Unions are about social justice. We strive for that as a collective. We challenge social injustice – poverty, inequality – because we know it damages individuals, families and communities and the whole of society. The STUC Women's Committee also know that poverty disproportionately affects women and that is a real concern for us. If women are experiencing poverty, so are their children.

In two thirds of the homes experiencing poverty, at least one adult is working. That's telling us something about pay and conditions for a large section of the workforce. It tells us too many workers are being paid poverty wages and that isn't acceptable to trade unions, which are about driving up living standards for workers. A by-product of this is that children are going hungry. Because of these economic realities, we need government intervention, and one of the ways of extending the safety net is the provision of free school meals. That's why the STUC and the Women's Committee and unions like the EIS are at the vanguard of this.

The battle of Kenmure Street

Anonymous

In May 2021, activists, trade unionists and others came together to try and halt the removal from a Glasgow flat of two Indian men by Home Office enforcement officers for alleged immigration violations. The speaker – a trade unionist himself – wished to remain nameless on the grounds that events that day were about collective action and not individuals.

THE NO EVICTIONS NETWORK was put together to resist a policy where the Home Office was switching contractors for its accommodation provider for people in the asylum system. As part of this, through a series of Byzantine procedures, the existing contractor was going to be changing the locks on a bunch of people. That was obviously not good for anyone. The No Evictions Network originated in order to challenge this via a legal framework or blockades and doorstep defences.

When Covid hit, it evolved to resist the dispersal of people in the asylum system for different reasons, where you had people taken out of their home accommodation and warehoused in hotels. So people who were already experiencing trauma from being displaced were once again being displaced. This had horrific consequences with a violent incident in a hotel in Glasgow in June 2020, so things were pretty raw coming off the back of that.

The Network had been tipped off that in the wake of Covid restrictions easing, there was going to be a rise in the number of Home Office removals taking place. We started laying the groundwork again to be able to spot those and defend against them and make sure people knew their rights. We hadn't expected to actually catch them in the act and block a van.

By pure chance, the previous evening, me and a few other people from Glasgow had been attending an online skill share training session with a different migrant rights group specifically focusing on what to do if you happened to encounter a raid in action; this is the game plan, this is what you can do from a legal standpoint. It showed materially how to manage that situation if it happened. But we were talking entirely hypothetically. We had no idea that the very next morning we would need to employ all of this.

That day, the playbook was exactly as we'd discussed it the previous night. We had an existing network of text notifications and group chats in order to alert one another to any sightings of enforcement vehicles around Glasgow. Primarily this was in case of enforcement officers questioning people and doing spot checks, so we could let people know about their rights. But in this instance, I was sitting at my kitchen table having breakfast and it popped up on the group chat that a raid was in progress on Kenmure Street. There was a picture of the van, this person was keen to tip us off and get people down there. They said that the officers were already in the building where the people lived, so time was of the essence. We were to spread the word as quickly as possible.

I threw my jacket on, jumped on my bike and pedalled furiously. I arrived and saw some men prowling around the flat looking down at us and the van was parked outside. Then there was a tense ten minutes or so, a window of tension, where I was there by myself waiting for other people to arrive, hoping that the van wasn't going to disappear before they did. People were walking past, coming back from the school run or shopping, and I was pointing out what was happening and urging them to let their neighbours know. Slightly further down the street, people were observing prayers, so I went to tell them and came back as quickly as I could. The idea was to raise the alarm. The more people who knew could tell other people, even if they weren't able to stick around.

I decided to try and get into the building and see if I could talk to the people who were being removed. I had no idea whether or not the enforcement people would let me in, but in this instance they let me into the stairway and I was filming on my phone. They wouldn't let me into the flat itself, and so I couldn't see the men or talk to them or gauge the situation. It was tense but quiet. A couple of neighbours poked their heads out to see what was going on. I told them and they were horrified.

Eventually the enforcement officers led these two guys out and it was a narrow stairwell so I had to back down in front of them, trying to keep filming to get as much evidence as possible in case it was useful to their lawyers later. At that point going down the stairs felt like crunch time. I backed out on to the street and one other person had arrived. I don't know her name, but then this whole day was about strangers turning up for one another with no context beyond knowing that another person needed you. I saw this lady and I knew there were only 10 or 20 seconds before the enforcement officers were going to come out of the front door. I simply said to her, 'Give me a 30 second head start and then I want you to tell them that there's someone under the van.' I told her to start filming then I nipped around the other side of the van so they couldn't see me and crawled under. And that was pretty much my day until 5.30pm!

It wasn't a spur of the moment decision. This was something we'd talked about the previous night as well. We weren't recommending doing this, and it was a high-risk strategy, but I knew it was a useful tactic. It was worth it, particularly in terms of buying time for people to get there. It needed doing.

My head was directly under the tyre so I couldn't see anything. When friends and people from the Network started arriving in numbers, they set up directly behind the van, a few feet away from me, and we were able to talk a little bit, though I didn't have much to report from down there. They gave me a running commentary and dealt with the police and the enforcement team responses in so far as they felt they needed to.

Perhaps around 10.30am, someone arrived on the scene who was a trained nurse and she was great with keeping me appraised about what was going on around me and checking in to remind me to move my fingers and toes so I wouldn't get nerve damage. I couldn't lift a cup or a water bottle under the van, so my friends scratched around and between them and located a CamelBak water bottle and lobbed a hose under the truck for me to suckle on. It was pretty tight in there – I couldn't lift my phone up to see it, so all of this had kicked off and it was only when I got home afterwards that I was able to go on to Twitter and find out what happened.

I took things moment by moment. I assumed that at best I was going to spend a night in the cells and was reconciled to that. I didn't for a moment imagine that we'd win, if I'm honest. I was holding out for a strategic victory – the longer that we delayed the van was time that it was kept away from detaining other people. Buying time was the goal.

Then at about 5.30pm, the lawyer Aamer Anwar ducked his head under the van and said 'Hey, they've said they're willing to let these guys go if you get out.' I crawled out and in the moment was really worried I was going to accidentally bump into some cop's boot while crawling out and then get done for assault! Aamer asked them to stand back, I crawled out and had a massive headrush, I was so dizzy. I was dazed and euphoric. There was this huge roar and we were all grinning like idiots. The two men were not going to be taken away.

One of the gang spirited me off down a side street before the police could change their minds. We disappeared down the alleyways and I found somewhere to finally go to the toilet. There was a three-minute interval where I felt like a hero and then someone came out of their house to tell me off for pissing up a wall. So that was humbling.

I'm thrilled that unions and trade unionists throw their weight into these actions now, but I'm also keen to acknowledge that unions are not immune to some of what has happened in the past. I think we have to directly acknowledge the complicated history of Britain's unions as bastions of both racism and anti-racism; that our tradition has also been one of white supremacist bargains in lieu of true working-class solidarity. The 1919 Glasgow strikes secured the 40-hour working week. We can't understate that victory, but nor should we overlook the fact that our unions chose to secure that win by stoking race-riots against black and Chinese workers and then wielding that unrest as a bargaining chip in the negotiations.

Imagine explaining to its architect Manny Shinwell that a century later, his counterparts would put their bodies on the line at a moment's notice to keep two South Asian men safe in their homes. Anti-racist action isn't just a moral obligation for our unions; it's a matter of historical course correction too. As the song goes, *Which Side Are You On?* I think for unions to be strong they have to be strong in their convictions as well as strong in numbers.

Apartheid, Mandela and Scotland

Brian Filling

Throughout South Africa's Apartheid era, Brian coordinated opposition in Scotland, campaigning alongside fellow trade unionists and other activists. Afterwards, he was appointed Honorary Consul for South Africa in Scotland. He is now Chair of Action for Southern Africa Scotland, and of the Nelson Mandela Scottish Memorial Foundation.

MY GREAT-GRANDFATHER WAS a delegate at the first Congress of the STUC and my grandfather used to take me to the Socialist Sunday School. He was also a trade unionist, of course, as were my parents. At the Socialist Sunday School speakers would come along and tell the children about various things – the railways and other things kids would be interested in – but they also talked about socialism and trade unionism, so that was my early introduction to politics.

They got children to do various jobs and at nine-years-old I took the meeting minutes! My grandfather did talks around the Socialist Sunday School groups and he used to take me as his assistant. He would do a variation of the *Ragged Trousered Philanthropist* 'Great Money trick'. He was a sheet metal worker and would ask the children, 'So what do you find in a town?' They would say 'a factory, a school, a hospital' and so on. At that time, they would also say 'a pawn shop'!

He would build these things in sheet metal in front of them then we would give them cardboard, rulers, scissors and glue and they would pretend to be working in a factory making boxes which they'd present to us. He'd give them a Farthing for each box, with which they then could buy little bottles of lemonade and biscuits. By the end of it all they had drunk all the lemonade, eaten all the biscuits and we took back the means of production (rulers, scissors and glue) and so we had all the boxes, tools and money. It was a good explanation of how things worked and still work in terms of capitalism and class. That was my introduction to capitalism and the need for trade unions and socialism, and of course when I started working I got directly involved in a trade union.

My political principles, my understanding about capitalism, colonialism and imperialism meant I got involved in all sorts of issues throughout my life. The anti-apartheid campaign was part of that. When I was a student at Glasgow University debates were a big thing. A thousand students would turn up. My maiden speech was in a debate where the motion was to stop Britain sending arms to South Africa. Apartheid was a big issue, as were other international issues, especially Vietnam. There was also the struggle to save UCS.

I went to London to become editor of the Young Communist League paper, *Challenge*. I got to know a lot of the African National Congress (ANC) people while I was there. They were in exile, of course. I came back to Glasgow in the mid-'70s and I got involved with Portuguese and Spanish solidarity. I brought a lot of anti-fascist activists from Portugal and Spain to speak, including to the STUC Congress.

I got involved in the anti-apartheid movement. There wasn't enough coordination, so we came to the conclusion that it needed to be better coordinated, and we set about doing that. We founded the Scottish Committee of the Anti-Apartheid Movement in 1976. That coincided with the Soweto Uprising. I became the founding Chair and remained Chair until the end of Apartheid in 1994.

Opposing Apartheid was a consequence of my political understanding. I always saw the issue of capitalism and imperialism as a global thing. A victory somewhere else in the world was as close to me as it would be if, for example, the shipyard or bin workers won in Glasgow. I didn't really make much distinction. It was the same enemy. That helped me to explain to people why their issues should be seen in a global context.

The ANC had called for a boycott of South Africa in 1959 and this led to the creation of the Anti-Apartheid Movement. It took the form of the consumer boycott, and things like sport, cultural and academic boycotts. Everything, eventually. That ran through the whole campaign. There were big events interspersed as well, and here the Free Mandela Campaign became central. That originated because Glasgow was the first city in the world to give Freedom of the City to Nelson Mandela in August 1981. We got quite a bit of stick for that because Mandela was described as a 'terrorist' by the Thatcher Tory government and the media.

In 1984 we organised a delegation of UK mayors led by the Glasgow Lord Provost in their gold chains, ermine furs and hats to 10 Downing Street to protest against Apartheid and call for the release of Mandela. Mrs Thatcher remained unmoved. Then in 1986 we renamed St George's Place 'Nelson Mandela Place' and that captured the imagination as we'd been picketing the South African Consulate which was on the fifth floor of the stock exchange on that street for years. Between 1985 and the 1986 re-naming, we had a weekly picket there, mainly staffed by shop steward committees. The trade unions were great supporters of our campaigns which included Aberdeen awarding the Freedom of the City in 1984, Midlothian District in 1985 and Dundee in 1986.

Next came the 1988 campaign 'Free Mandela at 70' with a demonstration and rally in Glasgow, from Kelvingrove through Nelson Mandela Place to George Square and on to Glasgow Green. There was a huge rally of 30,000 people addressed by Oliver Tambo and 25 marchers were sent off to London for a rally in Hyde Park.

Glasgow was designated the European City of Culture in 1990. We used this hook to hold the Sechaba International Conference and Festival: Cultural Resistance to Apartheid. Campbell Christie [former STUC General Secretary] was one of the people on Sechaba's Board, which I chaired. We used to meet in the STUC offices. It was an amazing event. We ran comedy nights, a folk song week, films, a nightclub, a writers' night, exhibitions and the first performance of a piece of music by Bill Sweeney based on a poem by Mongane Wally Serote. Govan Mbeki, who had recently been released after 25 years in jail, was the keynote speaker at the conference and the Guest of Honour at the concert.

All of these events were the background to Mandela visiting Glasgow after his release. I was appointed as coordinator for his visit. On 9 October 1993 the nine UK cities which had given him Freedom of their cities came to the ceremony in Glasgow.

Afterwards a huge rally was held in George Square. I took him to Nelson Mandela Place. The idea was we'd drive through, but he wanted to get out and look at it. You could see people thinking 'Is that Nelson Mandela?' He found it quite amusing to see a street named after him when I explained about the Apartheid Consulate being there. I spent the whole weekend with him. The following year I was invited as a guest to his inauguration as President of South Africa.

A lot of people thought Apartheid ended when Mandela was released from prison in 1990. That wasn't the case, as he made clear when he spoke at the Wembley concert after his release. The struggle continued – the Apartheid regime hadn't agreed to elections. In fact, between his release and the eventual election in 1994, 10,000 people were killed. There was a proxy war by the Apartheid regime to stir up trouble and derail the negotiations. Mandela's release was a staging point on the road to the end of Apartheid, but not the final victory.

Apartheid ended in 1994 with the ANC being elected and Mandela's inauguration as president. Later that year, we took a Scottish delegation of 33 people to South Africa, including six members of the STUC General Council. We took another delegation in 2000 and a section including Bill Speirs [then STUC General Secretary], visited the Northern Cape. The big issue we were campaigning on at that time was asbestos, the role of Cape PLC and the campaign for compensation. There were asbestos dumps that children were playing on and Bill brought a big bit of asbestos back to demonstrate that. The trade union movement had always been linked, right from the start, with our campaign. We brought many people from the ANC and the South African Congress of Trade Unions to the STUC.

The new South Africa brought dignity to the vast majority of the population with the ending of Apartheid. That was a great victory, but of course there are the legacies of colonialism and Apartheid which cannot be overcome in a short time. There are still many difficulties, so while there are victories, *a luta continua!*

Freedom From Fear for shopworkers

Caroline Baird

Caroline began working for Tesco in 2007 and joined Union of Shop, Distributive and Allied Workers (USDAW). She later became a rep and an enthusiastic champion of the Freedom From Fear campaign, which highlights the abuse of shopworkers by customers, and helped bring about a new protective law in Scotland.

WHEN I WAS working on nightshifts, I was physically assaulted on the shop floor. I was covering the self-scanning machines helping people put their shopping through. We could also serve self-scanner customers cigarettes, from a cabinet, and I was doing that. If I hadn't bent down to get to the cupboard, I would've been hit square in the head with an ironing board. It wasn't being aimed at me, but two drunk guys who had come in were carrying on all around the shop after grabbing the ironing board. One of them threw it through the air, presumably to hit the other guy, but he moved out of the way and it hit me on the back. If I'd been standing, it would have hit me in the front and floored me.

That made me think a lot about the verbal and physical abuse that we took as shopworkers. Even though it wasn't aimed at me that time, a lot of customers came into the store and aimed abuse at us. That happened especially when it came to 'Think 25', for alcohol sales. If we don't challenge customers and ask for ID for their age, it's us that can get a criminal record, not the customer, not anyone else. And that can affect your future employment.

So I'd seen and heard the physical and verbal abuse that colleagues got, received some of that abuse myself, and that made me want to campaign for change through the union. We are some of the lowest paid workers and we get most of the abuse. You should never feel under threat when you go to work.

The Freedom From Fear campaign has been going on for a long time. We campaigned in store, a public-facing campaign at the front of the store or in the car park. It wasn't just for union members that worked in Tesco, we were engaging with customers, saying 'Do you know this is happening?'

We campaigned for a bill in the Scottish Parliament, and that finally came into being in August 2021. It meant it was a criminal offence to physically or verbally abuse a shopworker. By now, I was seconded to work for USDAW full-time, and so I was going around all of the supermarkets, and they all got behind the campaign. The employers were supporting the staff and working with the union, which was great, and obviously doesn't happen all the time. Together we were making customers aware that the new law had come in. Most of them said: 'Oh my God, was that not a law before?!' The public support was great.

Fast food workers rise up

Claire Peden

Having long been interested in workers' rights, Claire attended a short union course and immediately became an activist. An organising role with the Bakers' Union followed, and she helped mobilise fast food workers, not least when 2018's 'Beast from the East' storm struck.

THERE IS AN imbalance when you think about bosses compared to workers. A lot of issues, people say 'Oh that's just the way it is.' But that's down to education – I didn't learn anything at school about my rights and about unions, I learnt nothing until I looked it up myself. So a lot of people go through their lives thinking that we just have to put up with things. The media teaches us that too. It's always against the worker. Once you realise that together we can be stronger and we can make changes, you will never let that go.

Me and some other activists had finished a small project in colleges talking to young workers about their concerns and I'd been doing some work with the STUC, but we were a little bit in limbo. Then the Bakers' Union took us on with a part-time, temporary contract to do special projects, mainly speaking to workers in fast food outlets about their issues at work.

Working with the Bakers' Union alongside the STUC was the first real attempt at trying to organise fast food workers in Scotland. We spent every day going around KFCs, McDonald's, Dominos just building up some trust with the workers. There were lots of issues around low pay for young employees and staff turnover.

The culture we were fighting against was difficult – access to the sites was almost impossible. We got thrown out and banned from so many McDonald's it was ridiculous. It got to the stage that we were waiting in car parks, trying to talk to workers on their breaks.

Things haven't moved on massively in those sectors, but we were able to get our feet in the door and start organising workers. I know some of the workers that we talked to at the very early stages are still trade unionists and are organising their own workplaces. In some places we got whole groups of workers joined-up and organised, and that was most definitely down to those people who worked on these sites.

In February 2018, we were carrying that on with some young workers in Livingston, talking about the usual things around strength in numbers and organising. On the morning when the snow came on really heavily, we texted our workers and said 'Stay safe' and 'Is your work closing?', just the usual checking-in with people. As the day developed we had correspondence from a worker at the McDonald's site in Livingston, and he had said that the store was still open. There were no customers, and the restaurant was cold. We phoned back and said the first step is to speak to your manager and explain that you feel unsafe.

This was going on for a while with a back and forth with the manager. The manager had called a senior manager who said not to close the store. The worker started to get concerned because public transport had stopped and it was becoming apparent that workers in the retail park would have no way of getting home.

The worker spoke to his colleagues who all agreed there was no need for them to be there and it was becoming dangerous, and that they needed to start the long walk home. We helped him write a letter that another union member who lived locally printed and got through the snow to McDonald's and passed to him. It said that if they did not close the store, they were effectively going to withdraw their labour anyway. He and his colleagues signed it, and they took it to the manager. He agreed they could go home and that the store would be closed.

The worker didn't just leave it there. He went across to KFC on the same retail park and helped the workers in there do exactly the same. They staged a walkout, basically. And that was that: the workers walked off home. They felt empowered. It was the first time they had done anything like that.

Afterwards, KFC refused to pay those other workers. We went straight back in there and got everyone together. We called them out publicly and within three days they had agreed to pay every worker for the store being closed. Every time there is a win, it inspires someone else to fight back and to challenge their bosses.

One thing I love about the STUC is that they give young workers a chance through their projects to experience what it is like to be part of an active trade union, and to engage with things they want to fight for. Straight away, you feel like you belong, and that you are part of something.

Opposing dockyard privatisation
Colm McConnell

In the mid-1980s, the government pushed to privatise Rosyth's Royal Dockyards. They met resistance from trade unionists including Colm, then working in the yard's accounts department and serving as union branch secretary. Even in eventual defeat, there were lessons and gains.

IN THE TORY government of the time, Michael Heseltine was the Secretary of State for Defence. He appointed this guy, Peter Levine, who actually had a defence company, to help with defence procurement and basically he was going around advocating privatisations everywhere. He was employed directly by the Ministry of Defence and he wrote a report on the Royal Dockyards. He was supposed to consult with the trade unions, and he did so, but we found out later from a leaked document that he had handed in his report to the Secretary of State before he'd even spoken to any of the trade unions, so it was obviously going to be a *fait accompli*.

Levine made his report and shortly afterwards the Government published the Dockyards Services Bill, a Bill which was only four lines long. They had real difficultly with the Bill – it took them four years to get it through parliament. When you consider some of the massive privatisations that have happened that went through in a matter of weeks or months, that must tell you something.

In terms of actions to oppose the privatisation, we did everything you can think of. There were local petitions. We commissioned an academic to write a book. One of the arguments we made through that was that we should move away from yearly budgets given that some ships take three or four years to refit, and towards a more commercial way of financing work. But of course they didn't pay any attention; they just wanted to go ahead and privatise. That was the whole thing with that Tory government: privatise everything.

Despite us providing an instructive and sensible vision in that book, it was just ignored. We then had lobbies of Parliament, although I can remember the BBC commentating on one of them, and they described it more as a 'Work's outing' rather than a lobby of Parliament! There was about 800 of us who went down to London that day. There was a big rally held in the Albert Hall with pipers, so I suppose that gave an impression of a jamboree rather than a lobbying.

It was probably obvious that the privatisation would go through, but we had some success in delaying it, especially through lobbying. There were two people in particular in the House of Lords who were interested in it – Baroness Vickers and Lord Denning, the former Master of the Rolls. He had a personal interest in the dockyards. With his legal mind, he was extremely unhappy with the original Dockyard Services Bill, especially because what it wanted to do was keep the dockyards and all the assets of the dockyards still in government hands, but employees would be handed over to whichever company won the contract to administer the dockyards.

So Lord Denning started to argue this concept that we were the bees in the hive, and you couldn't just move the bees without the hive or vice versa. This bees and hive argument took off, and won a fair amount of support in the House of Lords. The Bill itself was having difficulties getting through. There were issues over national security – you couldn't have foreign ownership of any of the companies involved. All these sort of issues began to come out and were key reasons in why it took four years to privatise us from a four-line Act.

We noticed that Lord Denning would argue more in favour of the person he'd spoken to last, so the unions would try to corner him immediately prior to any debate in the House of Lords. That way the last thing he'd have in his head was arguments from us. The civil servants were the same – they would hang on to him and not let him speak to us.

Though we lost in the end, there were long-term victories of solidarity. When you looked at the organisation of the civil service, we were split into industrial workers and staff, and we had separate national bargaining. But the dockyard campaign was the first major campaign where industrial workers and staff were all campaigning together. They had come together in the NHS and in GCHQ for one-off days of action, but the anti-privatisation campaign, being the size it was really brought the two sides together for a sustained period. It didn't stop the industrial stewards calling me a 'management bastard', mind, but the point was that staff and industrial workers got together far more closely.

When the privatisation inevitably happened, that closer affinity helped us greatly when it came to dealing with the new employer.

Call Centre Collective

Craig Anderson

When the Covid-19 pandemic began to afflict the country, working conditions changed. For some, there were new threats to health and safety, and technological concerns. Communication Workers Union (CWU) Regional Secretary Craig helped call centre workers find their voice and challenge wrongs.

IN THE CALL centre industry, there is a lot of precarious employment. There are companies who don't follow proper processes, don't have adequate health and safety and can really take advantage of the work force. That became a real focus during Covid, when we decided to establish the Call Centre Collective.

I've always been a big supporter of the STUC's Better Than Zero (BTZ) campaign and we've had BTZ give presentations to young workers. What they do is unique. What happened was that during lockdown, BTZ were getting an awful lot of enquiries from workers in call centres. I agreed with the STUC that we at the CWU would pick up some of them and work with the people making them. These people enquiring weren't trade union members. There were more and more enquiries from certain workplaces, especially call centres. I've had experience with many call centres so I was able to contact a few different people and see what we could do about it – how we could actually represent the underrepresented within the call centre industry.

We decided we would do that by creating the Call Centre Collective (CCC), where people from different unions, the STUC and other campaigners and researchers would work together to actively look at what they could do to help workers in these places.

It was a case of gathering information and putting information out, and trying to get bad practices stopped and highlighted.

Apart from helping individuals with their queries, we had a few big successes. For example, we came across one workplace where they were still being asked to attend work, rather than work from home. We highlighted that and it changed.

Then there was a company, Teleperformance, who had notified their employees that they were going to get webcams. These webcams were described as voluntary to start with, and only for team meetings. But if you investigated Teleperformance's website and what they claimed they could do with webcams, and what they are doing with webcams in some countries, it became apparent to us that these webcams had AI and would be used to monitor employees' movements and to actually monitor their production, effectively. That also became apparent from speaking to some employees, who were very scared to come forward as they knew they would be dismissed.

We contacted the *Daily Record*, the *Daily Record* took the story on, and it went front page, at which point a few people in that company were not too happy with us. But these weren't false allegations. We had the internal memos to back it up. We had made sure that everything that was said was correct.

Also, they were taking people on and asking them to use their own homes and their own equipment. I think that's where there's now a danger of exploitation of the workforce, where companies are effectively saying 'Yes, you are an employee, you do work for us but we don't need to supply anything for you, we don't have to support you in any way, we have no responsibility for you. But we want to monitor you ten hours a day, sitting in your house.' That's absolutely unacceptable.

The story broke at the start of the week, and by the Friday it had been withdrawn.

The CCC met as a group a few times a month. We reacted to situations. People joined the union. We recommended other unions too if they were the recognised ones for those workplaces. We also worked with a lot of people who weren't trade union members. That was the difference – some unions say: 'Unless you're a member, we can't do too much.' But we took some of the ethos from BTZ and went with what was happening at the time and tried to be quick in responding to it.

Direct action and groups like CCC and BTZ are a way forward to breaking that barrier and showing workers who probably don't know a lot about trade unions that there are people out there who want to fight for them. And that if they do get together, they can work as a collective and make real changes.

UCS work-in

David Cooper

When the liquidation of the Upper Clyde Shipbuilders consortium of yards was announced in 1971, shop stewards organised a famous, victorious work-in. One such steward was David, a marine engineer at Yarrow's.

I WAS AT sea when the work-in started and Jimmy Airlie and me came back to help – not that I've got any special qualities, Jimmy just knew that I knew the industry intimately, and he was anchor of the campaign.

The yards had a full order book but a profound cash crisis. Eighteen months before the bankruptcy, the government advanced £9m to cover the deficits, but the point was the money that was advanced was not nearly enough to cover the problem. So all you were doing was delaying the problem until the next cashflow crisis. The mood of the workforce in general was that the closure was completely unacceptable, and that we'd fight.

The atmosphere was one of solidarity, that was always the same in the shipyards. It was something akin to the miners. We were a family. In the event of problems we acted together. The atmosphere in that sense was positive, though obviously we were facing a very difficult time.

There were two massive demonstrations throughout Glasgow and they culminated in the traditional place of Glasgow Green. People reckoned there was 100,000 there. Shop stewards and workers came from all over the UK and Ireland, and some people from abroad came to support us and most of the English companies bidding for the yard sent up delegations, and promises of financial support. The campaign was run on the basis that everyone was welcome regardless of their political affiliations, as long as they shared this common objective – to save the yards. The SNP were represented on the platform by their General Secretary, Billy Wolfe. During the course of his remarks, he started criticising the English, which was quite frankly bizarre. Jimmy Airlie ordered Wolfe off the platform. So that took care of that.

I was there for the famous 'nae bevvying' speech. Jimmy Reid and Jimmy Airlie were both very fine speakers. Jimmy Reid was spokesman for the campaign, and there was a perception in the Clyde area that shipyard workers liked a drink, and in some cases it went a bit far. Jimmy acted to dispel that completely and made his point that there would be no drinking, and that would not be tolerated, and there was absolutely no problem during the campaign with drink.

My role in the campaign was that I worked in the machinery installation department – I was an engineer but that's what I was trained to do originally. I was elected a shop steward though I should emphasise I'm a very ordinary punter. Indeed Jimmy Airlie was the convenor of the engineering union, the EEU. So I became one of Jimmy's shop stewards. My role in that sense was to protect Jimmy's back.

In the end, we undoubtedly won a victory, though it wasn't an easy passage. There were interruptions during the course of the campaign and equally the official trade union movement announced in a meeting that they were now going to take over the running of the campaign. Jimmy Airlie, who was Chairman of the Joint Shop Stewards' Committee, told them in no uncertain terms that they would not be taking over the campaign and the shop stewards and workers would continue to lead it – we were doing very well so far and would continue to do that. We appreciated any help forthcoming from any quarters, but nevertheless, the decisions would be made within the organisation of the yard.

It was a long arduous campaign, I'm not suggesting there weren't difficulties and crisis points during the campaign that had to be fought, for example there has always been differences between the outfitters of shipbuilding and the boilermakers. There were elements in the boilermakers who wanted to go it alone. Not a majority, but an influential minority.

Looking back now, there was a very deep feeling in the Clyde area that shipbuilding was part of our lifeblood, a tradition. Under no circumstances would we allow shipbuilding to go. Apart from that fact, it employed thousands of people. That mood ran through the whole community – shopkeepers, churches – they were all behind that view. The feeling at the end of the campaign was that it was a victory and everyone felt relieved and satisfied that the job had been done, and shipbuilding had been saved for the Clyde.

The campaign message to learn is that all workers should come together. There's a message for younger people during the times we live in now, when the working class has suffered – if you stand together, you can defeat very powerful forces.

1985 Teachers' Strike

David Drever and May Ferries

National trade union victories in the middle of the 1980s were hard to come by. Teachers in Scotland bucked that trend by achieving pay rises after years of real term cuts. Orcadian David and Clydebank-born May were teachers and reps who helped win this rare victory.

David: Trade unionism was in my blood, coming from a radical socialist family. My dad was an International Brigader in the Spanish Civil War. It was a topic of conversation at home when I was a child. I was aware of discussions of daily events in the news from the radio and then later on television. It was common currency in my childhood and growing up.

As a student I worked in Collins book factory. We didn't associate much with the full-time staff. In fact, we were looked at askance as we didn't pay tax, being students. The full-time staff were often disgruntled that we took home a bigger pay packet than them at the end of the week. They had a grievance about conditions and wages and were having a discussion with management. They weren't very well unionised and we happened to be sitting around and the manager was soft-soaping the staff he was talking to, making excuses for what was happening and trying to chide them back to work.

My natural sense of injustice at this kicked in and I took part in the discussion. I got an absolute roasting from the manager – 'How dare you join in, you're only a student?!' Funnily enough that seemed to light a spark amongst the full-time workers. They bristled, chipped in and took over. I stepped back and they gave this guy a good run for his money, and things got better after that. I had no involvement, but it did let me see, very simply and very quickly, tactics to divide people whose interests are in common, and also the strength of people when they find a way of standing together.

May: Growing up in Clydebank set a scene of trade unionism. The first campaign I remember being part of was when I started teaching. It aimed to achieve a class size maximum of 33. At a union branch meeting, I was exploring the arguments of why it was good for everyone. The Head Teacher was there as she was a union member. Soon after that, I asked her for a half-day off for a wedding. She absolutely went for me and catalogued all my shortcomings as a teacher and said I was only asking for a half-day because I was lazy. I was genuinely flabbergasted. She'd obviously got into her stride when the bell rang. The kids were back in the classroom and she just carried on. I was like a rabbit in headlights.

After a while, I said I couldn't stand any more of it and needed to go and see to my pupils, so I left. Colleagues asked me what had happened and I just burst into tears. I went home that night and told my dad this story. He said 'What were you doing in the room with her without your union rep?' And I said, 'Well I only went in to ask for a half day for a wedding, so I didn't know I needed my union rep with me.' He told me I needed to find the union. I did that, and it was the start of my activism.

David: There had been a steady fall in teachers' salaries through the 1970s and 1980s. The campaign that began in 1985 was spurred on by that, and by a very intransigent Tory government. It was, of course, pre-devolution, so while Scottish education was a Scottish matter, nevertheless the hand of the Westminster Tory government was quite strongly seen.

May: What tended to happen with teachers was that there would be a long period of no pay increases and you'd fall behind comparative workers. Then there would be an upsurge of feeling that something had to be done. Then there would be a period of actions.

David: The strike action itself began in late 1985 and carried on through 1986. We were very conscious that the circumstances we were working under in the mid-'80s were quite different from the heady days of the early '70s, where there was mass support for the action then, and the overall trade union movement was in a stronger position. In 1985/86, we were just in the shadow of the calculated defeat of the miners by Thatcher's government and it was quite obvious they were going to be intransigent in terms of what they were willing to negotiate on and offer.

We had to be box clever, and the campaign was based around targeted strike action and curriculum boycotts, tactics that allowed us to exploit the existing trade union legislation to get the biggest bang for our buck, so to speak. We were conscious that all-out strike would not appeal to the majority of teachers. Actions would have to be as targeted as possible, and those that were out would need their wages paid by those who were working, and we had built up beforehand quite a large war chest to help supplement that on the all-out strike action we took on several days.

May: By 1985, I was chair of my branch. There was a huge rally in George Square in December '85, full of teachers and school banners among the Christmas decorations. I was on the top of a double-decker bus that we used for speeches. That day was an amazing boost for people. We also went to London to demonstrate. On the strike days, there were also demonstrations as well, which added to a great feeling of solidarity. There were lots of different focuses for activity.

David: An important strategy we had at that time was to try and maintain public support as much as possible. It is a difficult thing to get the public in support of strike action, particularly when the vast majority of the media are hostile to that action. We met with a high amount of media hostility, but by and large we carried the public with us. I think there was perhaps a sense that there was an injustice going on. Also, education has played a curious role in Scottish culture over time. It's a bit like the NHS now – it has always been valued as being a 'good' in itself amongst the general public, and we were able to weave that into our campaign. So although it was a salaries campaign, we hammered home the point that this was for the good of Scottish education and the pupils we were teaching.

May: One reason strikes hit home was that suddenly parents had to look after their kids all day. But there was general sympathy for teachers. We still held a position of respect. Quite often parents' groups would be supportive of the claims. Politically that was a nuisance for the government as they couldn't set parents against teachers as such.

Because this was a teaching union, there were a lot of women involved. Historically, teachers had been well-behaved, 'respectable' women. You know, 'a nice job for nice girls.' But during the 1970s and 1980s, people from different backgrounds had been able to go to college or university and become teachers, and they often had different politics and were more activist. This riff-raff like me arrived with a different point of view and we were prepared to state what we thought and rock the boat. The 1985 action was part of that. Thinking back to that headteacher when I started, she was from that older generation and hadn't been used to people questioning her and asking for things. I could never have realised it, but she found me and this newer intake threatening. She saw trouble on the horizon.

David: We had unequivocal support from the STUC. That was valuable. It was very gratifying to teachers living inside their own bubble of teaching to see that trade unionists from quite different areas would come and support them and speak at rallies and public meetings and we had a lot of that. We campaigned amongst parent groups as well and had as broad a front as possible, but having the STUC support us with the organisation they were able to bring to it, and the very active and vocal support of other trade unions in the media and at meetings, was very helpful.

May: At that time, there was a Women's Committee at the STUC and there were lots of training opportunities through that. We were able to go on reps' training at the STUC which was brilliant because we met other people who worked in other sectors and it widened our experience so effectively. There was a really strong strand of women's activity – we met women who were active in unions dominated by men and faced far more daunting challenges than we did in the EIS. That was a real education.

David: It was a successful campaign. We won. We formulated a demand for an independent pay review. We wanted something that was not in the control of the Scottish Office, that is of the Tory government of the time, to dictate what would happen. We wanted a group set up that would be as independent as possible to determine what salary increase should be given, both for that year and to make up for the past years of declining salaries. The action became focused on the achievement of an independent pay review, and we got it. The result was substantial increases across the board along the lines of what we asked for.

There was a sense of satisfaction when we got our independent pay review at the end. We did, in that sense, manage to give the Tories a bloody nose. They learnt lessons and didn't allow that to happen again. We had exploited a way in which industrial action could be maximised at minimum cost. They changed the contractual regulations for teachers after that to ensure it couldn't happen again. But at that particular time it was a signal defeat for the Tories in a period when they were rampant after their success in the miners' strike.

Better Than Zero

Eilis O'Keefe

As a student, Eilis worked at Cineworld. A sudden shift in working conditions led her to engage with the Better Than Zero campaign and inspired continuing involvement with the trade union movement.

I KNEW ABOUT the STUC's Better Than Zero (BTZ) campaign for a few years before I got involved. Then in April 2018, there were some changes at Cineworld and that prompted me to get involved and join a union for the first time. I joined with a friend at work – it was us together, so we didn't feel alone, but we were singled out as the 'Union Goths', as they called us. I'm not even a goth; I just wear eyeliner sometimes.

In April 2018, *Avengers: Infinity War* had just come out and Cineworld took away our late night taxi policy, which was a big selling point of working there as it meant we got home safely during anti-social hours. It was prevalent for the *Avengers* film as we had a midnight screening where everybody finished work at 5am. When we woke up in the afternoon after getting home at 6am, we found out we'd had the taxi allowance taken off us.

Being aware of BTZ, we got in touch with them and that led to us having a meeting with some organisers and getting involved with BECTU, the union that represents cinema workers. We also got involved with the Safe Home campaign that BTZ were running. That went right across hospitality and tied us in with the Fair Hospitality Charter campaign too. It asked employers to sign up to this Charter that ensured that people who worked anti-social hours were getting transport home from work and that they were safe and weren't being put at risk.

We launched this big campaign within the cinema, so me and my friend trained as reps and attended STUC Take Control training. That helped us to start organising within the cinema. We launched a petition which ended up attracting the attention of senior management, which culminated in us having a meeting with a regional manager. We won back a proportion of the taxi allowance. That didn't go far enough, but it did motivate us to keep pushing because we saw what we'd already achieved.

From there I became more involved with the wider trade union movement and campaigns in other sectors – things like the Calling Out campaign the STUC ran about sexual harassment. I talked about that in the context of cinemas, and also went and spoke at an event at the Art School with Better Than Zero, making people aware of their rights at work. I was Chair of the BECTU young members' forum, I was branch co-founder and secretary for Cineworld BECTU and I was a delegate for the branch at the BECTU conference in 2019. At university I studied Music and I researched creative labour and musical labour, and did my dissertation on the Musicians' Union. So a lot of things happened following that one event in April 2018.

Joining a union, it is possible to achieve better conditions at work, that's the baseline. We achieved more awareness of our cause among members of the public and among colleagues of their rights. Our biggest tool has been social media – the trade union movement has to adapt to this new workforce with things like that.

Pharmacists prescribe change

Gordon Finlayson and Paul Flynn

The Pharmacists' Defence Association (PDA) is the STUC's newest affiliate and one of the country's fastest-growing unions. Gordon, a pharmacist and rep at Boots, and Paul, a former Boots pharmacist who recently joined the PDA staff, explain more and detail recent wins.

Gordon: It was late in my career that any sort of collective activity became an option – about 14 or 15 years ago. Then a couple of years in, the PDA offered training in helping colleagues who were facing difficult situations and I jumped at that chance. I felt that I was mature enough to have seen a bit that goes on in pharmacy, and how the big corporates treat individuals and can pick pharmacists off one by one. There was no collective voice for pharmacists at that time. I did that, and then I was asked by the PDA to stand for the Scotland and Northern Ireland regional committee.

Paul: There has been a big structural shift in how pharmacy operates. If we go back to the late 1800s and early 1900s, everybody that owned a pharmacy was a pharmacist. Generally, each chemist had one pharmacist-owner. So all of the negotiating bodies, all of the bodies that dealt with how the work got done, were based on owners. It was business owners rather than individual pharmacists that had a say on how things progressed and how they were done. As time's gone by, we've had the rise of Boots, Lloyds, supermarkets – multiples have become a big thing and it is now leaning heavily towards pharmacies being owned by these groups. The owners and the people in charge who make decisions are not generally pharmacists. That has coincided with some fairly detrimental goings on in the workplace.

Gordon: There are a lot of people out there who equate unions with the factory floor only, including within pharmacy. When you start communicating with pharmacists, you point out that one of the strongest unions around is the British Medical Association. But there is reticence from a considerable number of pharmacists over trade unionism. Plus, some pharmacists that are on the register are also business owners as well, so there is a bit of a conflict there. The PDA know that too, and you can't be a business owner and be a member. You have to be an employee pharmacist or a locum to be a member.

The big issue that we're working on at the moment is stress and wellbeing. The biggest issue that comes through the rep network is workload versus resource. All of the corporates talk about safe operating platforms and have processes in place with the theoretical aim of freeing up pharmacists' time. Unfortunately, that never seems to happen. We've done an industry-wide survey using the Health and Safety Executive's Stress and Wellbeing questionnaire which has shown some really insightful information into just how poor pharmacists are feeling at the moment. Covid has made things ten times worse – overnight, access to GP services became a lot more difficult, yet there was us on the high street, never closed, open throughout the pandemic, and in a lot of cases dealing with issues that shouldn't have come near us. It was very difficult for us to find anyone to refer people to.

Paul: We've run a number of campaigns recently. There was a violence and aggression campaign we supported alongside USDAW. We have campaigned on that on a number of fronts. We also have the Safer Pharmacies Charter where we encourage employers and others to sign up to seven basic standards of how pharmacies should operate. Sadly, none of the multiples have seen fit to get involved with that yet but we're working on that.

Currently, there's a sector-wide suggestion that there aren't enough pharmacists. That's a fallacy and we've pointed out several times that there are more registered pharmacists than there have ever been. But people don't want to work in community pharmacies (the pharmacies you see on the high street that provide NHS services) at the moment. They are so badly staffed, the conditions are so poor and you go into some places where they have maybe one or two members of staff, who only have a few weeks' experience and have no idea what they're doing, and you're expected to provide medicines safely and effectively to the 300 people who will come in that day. It is impossible. The stores are crumbling, the floors are covered in stuff. There are places you walk into and if it was a McDonald's you'd walk back out. It's frightening that employers and owners are able to get away with this. It's a risk to the individual pharmacist.

It's not safe and not good for patients or pharmacists. The multiples are saying there is a workforce crisis – not enough pharmacists to staff their businesses, therefore they say they are forced to reduce opening hours or close stores. They are basically trying to minimise their expenditure. The multiples are often owned by private equity groups who are asset strippers.

Gordon: The situation at Boots, where I work, that went on for many years was that the PDA realised that they had a substantial number of members there and they did what any union would do and asked for an official recognition agreement to represent pharmacists on a collective basis. Boots said no. There were various back and forth court cases and it went to the Central Arbitration Committee. The final outcome was that the PDA couldn't have a recognition agreement because Boots signed an agreement with the in-house staff association, the Boots Pharmacist Association (BPA). And they did that over a weekend. It was communicated through legal channels that the only way we could get recognition was if we had a vote to de-recognise the BPA. That could only be done if it was asked for by Boots pharmacists themselves. So six of us, including me, were signatories on the official request that went to the Central Arbitration Committee.

That started the ball rolling for a nine-month campaign. There was a huge majority to de-recognise the BPA. We did that, and Boots came back and said they would only recognise the PDA if we had a ballot saying people want you to represent them. So we went through a long and very active campaign – mailings, videos, a forum every day – and we won the second ballot with an even bigger majority. There was an astounding sense of joy at this. It was an outstanding achievement and from there we signed a recognition agreement, got a rep network in place and we're now into our third year.

One of the next steps was to go for recognition with Lloyds. Initially they were negative towards it but then they realised they were going to lose. Because of what we'd achieved at Boots, Lloyds actually sat down and agreed a recognition deal. Back at Boots, we've just completed our third round of negotiations over pay, and we can show to members that by being part of the PDA, you got more than every other salaried member of Boots got.

In the past, Boots pharmacists in Northern Ireland were paid less than pharmacists in the rest of the UK. They actually published a separate pay scale for Northern Ireland. We said that was not fair and they changed that. We also have an agreement from Boots now that as soon as they tell one of their pharmacists that they have to complete a piece of training, they have to provide resource for it to be done in the working day, or they will pay the staff member for doing it in their own time. That was not the case before. They are big gains. We're forever challenging them on equality issues – the gender pay gap and things like that.

Paul: It's a hopeful time, and an interesting and exciting one. We now have this voice and this capacity to enact change and have more say on how things go in our profession than we've ever had before. We have only just affiliated with the STUC, so getting more involved with union activity is on the agenda. It's really encouraging for the future of the STUC too that it can be 125 years old and still having new organisations affiliating.

Gordon: The PDA is the biggest pharmacist body in the UK now. We are 100 per cent on the pharmacist's side. We are not influenced by employers. We don't have to hold back from things that might upset them. We are taking on the mantle of being the pharmacists' representative body. The membership numbers show that.

Paul: We are expanding by roughly 10 per cent every year and have been doing that for a decade now. If that growth continues, by 2030 we'll have 80 to 90 per cent of the profession in the union, and we will hopefully have the influence that the BMA and the nurses' unions have.

Stopping NHS privatisation

Grahame Smith

Grahame was to become General Secretary of the STUC, a post he held from 2005 until 2020. Before that came more than two decades of trade union campaigning and work on many issues, one of which was the 1980s fight to stave off NHS privatisation in Scotland.

BY THE MIDDLE of the 1980s, we were having to deal with the real consequences of Thatcherism – the pressure on public services and the ideological attack on them with view to privatising them. As well as privatising, they had an appetite to marketise, creating internal markets in health and hiving off key parts to the private sector. Those issues concerned trade unionists, both those who worked in the NHS and whose jobs and conditions were under threat, but also more generally in terms of the maintenance of the NHS and effective publicly-funded, available at the point of need health services. That was the driving force behind the STUC's anti-NHS privatisation campaign, called the Scottish Health Service campaign.

As a student I worked part-time for the NHS and we were on strike the day I started. After university, I started work back with the NHS, driving an ambulance in Ruchill Hospital in Glasgow. I became a shop steward there and ended up joining the STUC Youth Committee. Eventually, an opportunity came up to run the Scottish Health Service campaign and I jumped at that. That was funded by the various health unions and donations from local branches, and COSLA encouraged their member Local Authorities to support us.

The campaign also had engagement with the voluntary sector and the wider public health sector. It linked into local health service campaigns and to the churches as well. They were often engaged by the STUC on campaigns that were about broader social policy areas. So the STUC hosted the campaign, employed the person running it and provided the admin support needed. I joined the STUC as a member of staff in the mid-1980s and didn't leave until I retired in 2020.

There was also a real effort to link in the campaign with local union branches and the trades council network. Some trades councils also set up their own local campaigns, mobilising with local people about local issues. My role was to support that kind of thing and give them access to contacts and resources.

We used petitions, letter-writing and lobbying health boards. We used opinion polls cost-effectively by tagging a couple of questions onto national polls – we asked the public whether they supported NHS privatisation and we knew we'd get a good result out of that, and then big publicity: '85 per cent of the public believe the NHS should be kept in public hands.' We had lots of local mobilising conferences and events, building up to lobbies and demonstrations. We produced leaflets for local distribution. Our slogan was 'Building Tomorrow's Health Service Today.' It doesn't sound very snappy now!

We were also keen to make the link with health inequality, so we did a lot of work around that, linking ill-health with inequality. We tied that into the wider agenda of the trade union movement – how good work is important to health, how reducing poverty and inequality has an impact on people's health. The campaign used those arguments and took a stand in raising the profile of that debate. We also got involved in wider debates about the future of the NHS, especially around provision of 'care in the community.'

It wasn't a hard task in winning the arguments. They were solid and sound and we had lots of public support. It was about finding lots of different ways we could keep the pressure and momentum up and keep the issue at the top of the agenda. We also linked it into wider issues that were being debated within society and the trade union movement, including constitutional things like devolution. All of that helped the campaign resonate with the public.

In terms of successes, we staved off some of the attempts to marketise the NHS in Scotland. That internal market didn't take off and didn't endure in the way it did elsewhere. But after the

1992 election, some services were privatised – cleaning, catering, portering. But the fact we kept the issues so far up the agenda was helpful in ensuring that there was a continued wider support for the Labour movement in Scotland over the period of the '80s and '90s, ultimately leading towards the election of a Labour government in 1997.

The relationship between the union movement and civic society and how that developed... I wouldn't say that what happened around the constitutional question was settled by what we did, but it was part of that way of working, where you brought together wider civic society to pursue common objectives. We used the same approach when we began the Scottish Pensioners' Forum.

These campaigns are important in mobilising the trade union movement at a local level, giving it something to be active around beyond the day to day negotiations over terms and conditions and dealing with the employer. We'd taken the trade union movement out to the community and made people aware of its relevance beyond the workplace.

If our objective was to protect a publicly-funded NHS available at the point of need, largely provided by public servants, then the campaign succeeded. We prevented what otherwise might have been a different outcome had there been no opposition to the Thatcher approach to running public services.

Responding to Piper Alpha

Jake Molloy

When the 1988 Piper Alpha disaster killed 167 men, North Sea oil rig workers turned their grief and anger into action. Jake was among those who formed the Offshore Industry Liaison Committee to push for change.

AT THE TIME of Piper Alpha, I wasn't active in a trade union. I was offshore, working on the Shell Brent Delta. The '80s were a time when the very mention of the words 'trade union' in the tea shack or anywhere else in the installation would very quickly see you run off – you'd be 'NRB – Not Required Back.' If you said anything which undermined a manager you were told to pack your bag and you were on the next helicopter.

That day I'd gone downstairs to make a phone call and I was passing the radio room at about 10pm and the radio operator said to me: 'There's something going on at Piper Alpha. There's word that there could be as many as six people dead.' I carried on, called home, asked my wife if she'd heard anything and she said there'd been nothing on the news. There was no television on the rigs or anything like that.

I came back downstairs and the operator said: 'It sounds pretty bad. People have been evacuated.' I went to bed and told the three guys I shared with before the lights went out. We got up the next morning to the full horror. But it didn't even hit home at that time. We were getting radio reports from BBC Scotland, but it was really two days later when the newspapers arrived and we were seeing images of the destroyed platform that it brought everything home. We all knew this was a dangerous industry, but we just could not comprehend the idea of so many deaths and an installation completely gone. And that was the catalyst to start trade union activity.

Piper Alpha triggered a reaction and workers found their voices across the industry. The horror stories began to flood in. It was a tidal wave of incidents and accidents, so many near misses. There was a complete absence of engagement with workers on day-to-day safety matters. That sparked in me the need to make a difference.

There was a guy, Ronnie McDonald, who had stopped a job on the Shell Tern Platform. He was quickly identified by workers as a candidate to take the lead. So he was put on a wage paid by contributions – guys chipping in a couple of quid to pay for his time and an office in Aberdeen. We were also cut loose by the mainstream trade unions at that time.

We had created this unofficial body that was taking all the action – the Offshore Industry Liaison Committee (OILC) – and it was an attempt to bring about a federal structure among the different trade unions. Our logo was based on the Polish *Solidarność* graphic – that was a bit of a joke of ours really as Thatcher had said that they were the type of trade unionists she could do business with. The thing was, we had that logo above the door of the office in Aberdeen, and we regularly got visits from Polish sailors and sea workers who thought it was some kind of club for them.

We did most of our organising and actions on the night shift. A lot of the time management would cut the phones in the daytime so you couldn't communicate, but you could at night. We did things in stages – one-day stoppages, two-day stoppages. They never knew when it was gonna happen because we would take action at the drop of a hat.

On the first anniversary of Piper Alpha, July 6th 1989, we stopped work across the entire North Sea for the day. That started things off. There had been a couple of events – for example, on January 1st 1989 the Brent Delta had a huge explosion, and but for the fact it was New Year's Day it would have killed a lot of people. Luckily, everyone was inside having a New Year's lunch. There was a tsunami of opposition and it triggered activists across the sector. They were queuing up to chair the next meeting. Big meetings were being organised in the cinemas and on areas of the platform. This rippled out across the North Sea, from the Brent up in the north down through the Forties Fields and the southern gas fields.

I very quickly took up the post of elected Safety Rep when the legislation changed in November 1989. That took me into trade union activity. Even then it was rare for union officials to get access to an installation. You relied on each other – that collective spirit of workers. We stopped the action late in 1989, and waited for the summer of 1990 because summertime was the period of high activity.

I was on £4.25 an hour in July 1989. By the time the stoppages had ended in September 1990, I was on £8.50 an hour. We worked out that the lowest increase for anybody in the oil and gas sector at that time was 47 per cent. Really, more than money the dispute was about health and safety. It was absolutely fundamental. Lord Cullen's inquiry came out at the end of 1991 and we had a voice now, and we were able to influence things.

Defeating university pension cuts in 2018
Jeanette Findlay

Standing together to protect pension rights is a seminal part of trade unionism. Jeanette was President of the Glasgow University branch of the University and College Union (UCU) when that sector's scheme came under threat.

WE RETAINED IN my part of the university sector a final salary pension scheme up until 2017. Then it moved to career average, which was something I felt we should have gone on strike about at the time. We were balloted, but we didn't get the numbers we needed. We went to career average but it was still a defined benefit scheme – you pay in, but you can calculate what you'll get, as opposed to a defined contribution scheme, which is where you pay in what they tell you and at the point you retire it is worth whatever it's worth. You're not able to plan, you can't say 'I'll retire now because I know I'm earning enough to meet my expenses' and all of that. It's a hugely inferior pension scheme.

In 2018, they were proposing that we went to a 100 per cent defined contribution scheme as opposed to a defined benefit scheme based on, at that point, career average. That was a massive detriment. It was hugely important and the turnout at branch meetings in Glasgow was massive when we were discussing this. People from the youngest to the oldest understood what a huge detriment this was. They understood this was a swingeing attack, not just a minor deterioration.

Pensions are complicated and we're talking about an intelligent workforce who are academic and academic-related. Even so, it's a difficult thing to explain, so there was a lot of effort at the start to try to distil it into what the essential points were. People generally don't really think about this. They think, 'I pay in my money, it gets taken off my wages.' You never see that money and you just know you've been told you're going to get a good pension. You don't think too much about it. There was a sudden realisation that you thought you had a contract with the university when you took up this job, which committed them to the form of pension that you were given, but you didn't. That was quite a shock for us all. This was a once and for all deterioration in terms and conditions that we would never get back, and we understood that.

It wasn't hard to mobilise people. There were endless conversations as we tried to get our heads around the changes. There were other changes too, but the key issue was the removal of the defined benefit scheme. We worked hard of course, but it was the easiest mobilisation I've been involved in. Prior to that, we had never had long strike periods. We were not a militant union that was used to taking big periods of strike action. It was incredible how we were able to do that, and it was the dead of winter when we went on strike in 2018. We did it in the form of two days one week, three days the next week, four the next and then five the next week. We were up to our knees in snow. Every day we expected that there would only be a few of us, and every day we had over 100 people, some days a lot more, at the main gate where we held the pickets. It was astonishing. In the end we did 20 strike days, that's a lot of money for people to give up.

There was an incredible atmosphere. It was the most unifying experience. All ages were there – really young graduate teaching assistants up to the top of the scale within both the administrative and the academic side. It was a huge range of people across all of the disciplines. People felt confident. A lot were picketing for the first time, so they were quite excited about taking a strong stand and being visible.

On the first day of the strike, the plan was that all of the striking workers in the Glasgow area would go to Buchanan Galleries steps and there would be a rally and some speeches. We had between 150 and 200 on our picket line that day, and we were going from the West End to the city centre. I said, 'Let's just rank up and march.' People were asking if we were allowed to. I said 'No', but pointed out that we were all going from A to B and it would be very unsafe for us all to try and fit on the pavements. We got the banner at the front – and ours' is an incredibly old one that is a nightmare to take anywhere – and we were all in yellow bibs, and we marched down University Avenue. We went through the park and onto Sauchiehall Street. As we got there, we had to turn left. I went into the middle of the road, stopped the traffic, and signalled everybody to keep going. Way down the road I could see two police officers who happened to be on patrol, walking along.

They saw this thing coming along, this mass of singing people, and they were trying to catch my attention, so I was waving back to them. They were heching and peching along, trying to catch up with us. They said, 'Erm, who is organising this procession?' I said, 'Oh no, this isn't a procession. This is just a lot of people going from one place to another at the same time.' They went, 'That's a procession.' I said it wasn't, and that there was a lot of us here so we were spilling onto the road, so it'd just be better if they stopped the traffic, because once we passed the junction, we'd be on a pedestrian precinct all the way to Buchanan Galleries. It was only two sections of road we were blocking. They said no again, they tried to negotiate with me, but everyone had continued walking and I was directing them through. So we got across and a lot of my colleagues were hugely delighted at just taking to the streets and having what they might've called an unlawful procession. I just called it a lot of people going from A to B at the same time.

On the daily picket lines, you knew you were standing with like-minded people and you could feel the strength of that. There's nothing like it. There were very creative placards, singing and me running up and down with the megaphone. Another thing that was great was having support from all the other campus unions, who we have a very good relationship with – Unison, Unite, GMB. Other trade unions like the RMT came along with their banners. Students mobilised and a big number of them came and stood with us and brought us hot drinks.

In the end, we won a huge victory. The offer that came in was essentially that we would not go to 100 per cent defined contribution. We went to defined contribution above £60,000, and that would be inflation proofed. We also agreed to set up a joint expert panel with trade union and employer representatives to talk about the valuation of the pension fund.

The victory that we achieved in 2018/19 was massive – despite what happened later. We stopped them in their tracks. It was exciting. Collectively exerting your trade union power and winning is deeply satisfying. There are lots of things about being an active trade unionist I like – I like dealing with personal cases, I like fixing things for people, small things that make people's lives better because they were part of a movement where they weren't on their own and somebody came and sorted something out for them. But there is nothing like exerting the collective power of your union to make a big difference like that.

Standing together for equal pay

Jennifer McCarey

In 2006, Glasgow City Council imposed on their workers a new pay grading system. Unions and their members felt that it was fundamentally flawed, not least in redressing the pay gap between men and women. Jennifer, Chair of Glasgow Trade Union Council and a Unison organiser, describes the drawn out but ultimately successful struggle which ensued.

THE COUNCIL WORKFORCE knew that the 2006 regrading had made very little difference in a lot of jobs. Many of the female-dominated roles in Glasgow had been contracted to arm's length companies like Cordia, who ran care, cleaning and catering services. With Cordia their over-time rate had been cut, they had lost holidays, they had lost pay increases. Discrimination didn't just continue in terms of them not getting the increase they should've done in 2006 to give them equal pay; their pay deteriorated because of structural decisions that were made to pay those workers less. They had seen their pay depreciate again and again. They had also been subject to some pretty horrendous management practices and policies.

Unions questioned the regrading scheme and the outcomes of it and decided to pursue a legal course against it. The law intervened at different times and unions were involved in testing what equal pay between men and women could and should look like in law. There were other issues to test too – if you were in an arm's length company that the council had set up, could you compare yourself to a regular council worker? Or did it mean you had no right to equal pay? So we then fought for the right for those people to be included.

It was a challenge to stay involved in the legal fight because it was expensive and time consuming. But ultimately, we felt that the way pay and grading in the City Council had been designed made existing inequalities worse, and contributed to women's pay being unequal. Eventually, a tribunal ruled that the City Council were unable to provide evidence that their scheme was equality proofed. Effectively that meant that they couldn't defend the current pay and grading system, and it meant that the pay and grading system would have to fall and we would have to renegotiate a replacement that was equality proofed. That rocked the bones of the council and had enormous consequences.

Lots of these groups of workers weren't very well organised. Many of them had turned their backs on unions. They felt they were in the pockets of management. We realised that this was a big opportunity to engage members and workers, and that they could be the agents of change and pursue the justice that was long deserved to them. Together, we set about developing an inclusive, open, democratic campaign that everybody who had an interest in equal pay could play a part in.

As part of that we started having big open meetings for the members. We also had a campaign day where we invited anybody who wanted to be involved to come and spend a day designing the campaign and starting a strategy so that it was member-led. Together we analysed what we needed to do, what our objectives were, who was with us, who was against us, who was in the middle, where the decision-making power in the council lay, and who we needed to engage with and talk to.

These are the women that keep our city going. They don't stop. They care for us, they look after the schools, they clean our care homes and nurseries, they look after every vulnerable person in the city and assist children in their learning. We knew the power that workforce had and if they worked collectively they could demonstrate that the city couldn't work without them, and that the city needed them.

There were a lot of smaller protests of 80 to 150 people, then in January 2018, they decided to hold a demonstration in the city. We all dressed as Suffragettes because it was the anniversary of the Representation of the People Act, when some women got the vote. We made all the hats and bands ourselves. The women led the demonstration and spoke at the rally. It was incredibly important and powerful. It was a big turning point as we got the attention of the press and the people of the city. After the Suffragette demonstration, the council said that they would no longer appeal the decision, and that they would begin settlement talks. So that was a really important victory.

The talks process was very difficult. It seemed to get nowhere slowly. It seemed to be an endless grind and the Council used stalling tactics. Our members quite rightly told us they were ready for strike action and that's what they wanted us to do. They could see no resolution otherwise.

In May, Unison and GMB did a consultation ballot on strike. At the last minute, the Council came to us with a proposal that they said would speed the negotiations along. So we agreed not to proceed to a formal ballot. That changed again in August when they decided to change the timescales on meetings and decisions. That was the point our members insisted on using strike action as a tool to demonstrate to the council that they were to be taken seriously. They came up with six demands which were made into a strike banner and logo by the artist Laura Miller.

The statutory ballot had an incredible turn out and a resounding yes to strike action, and we had a massive membership advance in that period too. The strike was set for October 2018 and the council walked away from the table when we informed them about it.

The strike was absolutely solid. We had around 8,500 on strike and 13,500 on the rally in George Square. We had more picket lines than I'd even seen before in the city. There were weans dressed in dozens of layers at 6am on the picket lines in that great tradition of mammies taking to the streets with their kids, as they had in many other disputes including the Rent Strike.

Amazing acts of solidarity sprang up – male refuse workers went into work and were picketed by the women, who cleaned those depots, and those men refused to take their vans out and they lost their pay. Glasgow Life workers refused to go in to work, car parking ticket people refused to go in. And the city was behind us. People lined the streets to clap us and every single person that the media went to interview said 'Good on them' and 'They deserve the money.' Many of the vulnerable that home carers looked after and their families came on our rallies because they wanted to show support. When they were asked 'Do you need care cover that day?', they said 'No we'll do it as we want our home carer to be able to go on strike.'

After that strike, things were completely different because the council knew that we would be out in a heartbeat. They knew that the women were not going to take anything other than a fair and reasonable settlement. And so the negotiations turned very serious and we started talking in the very business-like fashion that we had always known we needed to do in order to be sure that we secured all of our demands. We were able to sign off a deal before the end of 2018. Offers went out from January to May 2019 and pay outs went out from June onwards. We won £550 million.

Caterpillar lock-in

John Foster

It could be said that John's activism began in 1945 when, aged four, he wore a red tie while accompanying his parents to the polling station. A trade unionist all his life, he witnessed as an academic researcher the worker occupation of the Caterpillar factory in Uddingston.

CATERPILLAR IN UDDINGSTON had been opened in 1956 by a big American multinational that was developing plants for the manufacture of earth-moving equipment across the globe. They had around 30 factories and virtually controlled that entire market. But by the 1980s, it was running into trouble because of the growth of some competition and over-production, and the degree to which the world was moving into economic troubles in 1985.

Early in 1984, Caterpillar had agreed to massively increase the capacity of the Uddingston plant and develop a plan called 'A Plant With a Future'. This involved installing much more efficient, modern production equipment and the firm had gained a significant government grant to do so. They had a grand opening of the new facility in September 1985, something the Conservative ministers in Edinburgh were very grateful for given the industrial decline in Scotland then and the recession in the oil industry. There had been a continuing closure of Scottish plants at that time. Looking forward to a coming election in 1987, they wanted a good news story and so Caterpillar became very important indeed. Then, there was a change of policy and suddenly, in January 1986, management announced that the plant with a future was going to close.

As soon as workers got wind of what was happening, they decided they would occupy the plant. I think the name 'lock-in' came a little bit later. It was an echo of the work-in at Upper

Clyde Shipbuilders in the previous decade. But a work-in was not feasible at Uddingston because the plant depended on supply lines of imported components that were controlled by Caterpillar or its suppliers. The earth moving equipment it produced was also completed at other plants elsewhere. It would have been impossible to have done what was done at UCS, where they had all the necessary materials to complete ships.

The shop stewards at Uddingston therefore decided to play their strongest card. Occupying the plant, locking it, and denying access to management prevented the firm seizing the very valuable equipment that existed in Uddingston. And, to move it elsewhere, Caterpillar had to get it out of the factory. An occupation gave the workforce control and provided the stewards with a bargaining position. It was also inspired by two previous occupations that had been at least partially successful in the local area – one was at Plessey in 1982, and one at the Leyland plant in West Lothian. They had been successful, at least in stopping closure although there were some job losses. These victories gave the feeling that if the same tactics could be adopted, they could force the Caterpillar bosses in America to back down.

The key stewards – John Brannan and John Gillen – were amazingly good at projecting their message in a down to earth way that grasped the situation. It galvanised those working in the plant, it unified them and made them aware that they had a very good bargaining position, that it was worthwhile hanging on and defying this American company, but also it mobilised support in the surrounding community.

The leaders were able to maintain a remarkable solidarity for the 101 days the occupation lasted, to the beginning of March 1987. They also galvanised an enormous amount of solidarity from the immediate community, who went around collecting money – something like £20,000 per week. They also got support from other workers, including solidarity from the Golden Wonder crisp workers who also occupied when they were faced with closure around that time. There were great difficulties, of course. The white-collar unions decided that their members should withdraw. The workers were also under constant assault by the press who called on them to see sense and co-operate with management. And there were very difficult votes and arguments.

Despite the fact that there were pressures to capitulate, they were resisted and the lock-in was maintained. There was a legal attempt by the management to have the occupation ruled illegal and an interdict was granted, but the workers continued and they were able to cause a great deal of embarrassment to the Conservative government. It had been found out – Malcolm Rifkind had been there a few months earlier, celebrating this Plant With a Future, and he'd now been made a mug of.

The stewards showed great imagination in the ways in which they maintained morale. They managed to put together an earth mover which they planned to send to Nicaragua as an example of solidarity with a developing country that was at that time under enormous pressure from the USA.

They planned to transport it with the help of Oxfam and were all set to do so when they were stopped by a court action. Instead they left it bang in the middle of George Square, where it remained for something like three months! It was a symbol of their defiance of this American company and provided a centre point for their own financial collections, a symbol of solidarity.

In all these ways, they were able to sustain the occupation. The STUC, in particular Campbell Christie and his lieutenants, were able to galvanise very considerable support through the trade union movement right through that period. That lasted right up until the final days when a series of very close votes at mass meetings indicated that resistance would have to be maintained in different ways. However, the occupation ended in good order with an agreement forced on the company that an alternative plan would be sought with backing from a number of industrialists, the local authorities and the STUC to develop an alternative use for the site.

Ultimately this came to very little, but it did mean that the campaign was continued right up through the summer of 1987. That was important. It ensured that the Caterpillar closure, and the failure of the Conservative ministers in Edinburgh to do anything about it, remained a central issue in the election. It undoubtedly contributed to the Conservatives suffering in that election a cataclysmic loss of more than half their seats in Scotland.

What happened at Caterpillar in 1987 is to be applauded. It

wasn't an all-out victory because the American company did manage ultimately to retrieve its equipment and move it elsewhere and the plant was closed, and many people who had been employed there did not get re-employed. So materially the closure caused a great deal of suffering for people. But on the other hand, it was a massive ideological victory in terms of showing the ability of working people, without much experience of that kind of militant struggle, to come together and to fight a battle that had much wider political consequences and forced a massive American company on to the defensive, and played a big part in the defeat of the Conservatives in Scotland.

It also entrenched in the imagination of working people in Scotland that they were able to fight in the most difficult of circumstances for the objectives of public ownership, solidarity and the central role of the trade union movement. We are entirely correct to celebrate what was achieved by John Brannan and John Gillen and their colleagues in the factory at Uddingston.

Abolishing fire and rehire

John Kelly

John is a college lecturer and rep for the Educational Institute of Scotland/Further Education Lecturers' Association. In 2020, the terms and conditions of colleagues came under threat. In light of Covid restrictions, they used technology to fight back, an increasing trend in the modern trade union movement.

COVID WAS USED a lot by management in various industries as a cover for 'fire and rehire'. The trigger for our actions was what happened at Forth Valley college, where 30 or so college lecturers who were on lecturing terms and conditions were told that they were going to be made redundant but also told that if they went on to an alternative contract they would not be made redundant. That alternative contract removed them from the teaching contract which had much higher pay with a much better set of terms and conditions. A number of the staff there did concede and signed up for the new contracts, but a bunch didn't, and then that local branch went out on strike.

We as lay reps raised this in a national forum with college employers, and the employers told us at that meeting: 'Well, I think you should expect more of this across the country.' Deep down it was about trying to de-professionalise jobs to drive down pay. It then blew up into a national dispute because we refused to accept it and demanded commitments that it was not going to happen. We put a statement to them saying that they would reject fire and rehire, and no matter what you call a role, if the worker meets a profile they should get lecturing terms and conditions. They refused to do this and we ended up on a national strike.

Interestingly, a lot of the people who took strike action were not affected by what happened at that point. That showed the collective strength of the union. We fight for every one of our members. We don't simply fight when it's us that are in the frontline.

We eventually got a 100 per cent victory as they conceded on all counts including reinstating all of the former lecturers. And they agreed they wouldn't do this anywhere across the country, and we've got a process for dealing with issues which hopefully will avoid us having to take strike action in future. So all-in-all it was a complete and utter win, a resounding victory. The difference is striking, in more ways than one: those that do strike have strikingly better pay and conditions.

In that campaign we used modern technology a lot to get our messages across. That was something we'd been embracing since a pay campaign a few years earlier, and something unions increasingly are doing. Back then, we set up a Facebook page and a Twitter account, and when we had national negotiation meetings, we would give updates, sometimes during the negotiations, but always after we came out. So it wasn't a case of waiting for the newsletter or the meeting. People would know exactly what was happening in real time, almost.

Members loved that because there was a lot of connection there. I think a lot of unions recognise now that the days of sending out a newsletter or calling a conference alone are long gone. There is a need for all of these things, but you need to wrap things up into snappy short messages. Our attendance at branch meetings has gone up by staging them online as well. There is a great buzz in trade unionism over this new way of engaging. We need to embrace it and make the most of it. During the fire and rehire campaign, we had our socially-distanced picket lines, but we also had our virtual picket lines too. If you couldn't get along, you could support online. Some people sang along from there.

Of course, there are worries about isolation with that. It has been reinvigorating, but it shouldn't replace the real thing – we still need to meet together and stand together physically as well. Technology is just a great add-on.

There's nothing better as a rep than telling members you're going to win something for them and when you know they're right in their arguments. You know it's really worthwhile to do and that if we stick together we will do it. We need to work at increasing membership, but interestingly enough through Covid times union membership has not plummeted as some predicted. The union makes us strong.

Building a winning branch

John Neil

Assembling a union branch fit to fight against problems that are detrimental to workers' daily lives remains the heartbeat of trade unionism. The work of John, a cleaner at Glasgow University, demonstrates how this can be achieved to great effect in a modern setting.

TRADE UNIONISM WASN'T as strong as it could've been here at first. You saw people having trouble, moaning and niggling, and you thought: 'let's try and do something about this together, let's not moan'. The more senior reps mentored us and we made a more powerful collective from there.

The cleaners had issues like working with various chemicals that gave them psoriasis on their hands – they weren't treated well. The biggest thing was their contracts – they had no set amount of contracted hours and all seemed to be on different contracts to each other. It meant a lot of them had to work two or three jobs. But it was almost a forgotten section of the uni at the time. There was no trade union visibility. When issues started coming forward, at that point I realised: how many potential members are we looking at here? We had about 30 cleaners who were members at the time out of what could have been 350.

We spoke to the full-time officer and the organising team at Unite, and that's when you saw a totally different aspect. They were brilliant. They came in and did a reccy around the area to see what we were facing and what we were up against. They gave us the tools we needed to engage with the cleaners.

It was a case now of 'How can we get that visibility with the cleaners?' The cleaners didn't really have emails. Some had phones, some hadn't. It was quite a challenge. We realised we needed to go around, speak to them to get that visibility, hold meetings. That was the main thing. There is nothing that can be better for worker power than going to meetings together. Not emails. Communicate how they want to communicate.

We were there at whatever time they wanted to meet – half five in the morning, 11 o'clock at night. That built up a trust and built their confidence, because they were quite fearful of going to management with their concerns. At the first meetings, there was negativity, absolutely, against the union – 'We've seen it all before, the unions come in, the unions don't do anything.' That changed quite quickly when we listened to them and organised each section of cleaners into zones. Members and colleagues were coming forward, getting emboldened. They were thinking 'I'm in the union, I don't need to be fearful.'

We began with smaller actions and escalated it from there. There's no way you can go in there and say you want everyone to walk out and stand at the gates on strike. It's a case of building. We started wearing badges, we got them hats and wristbands. We said 'Right, these are your zones, whatever time you're starting at, you'll all go in with these wristbands on together. That gave them the confidence, as management noticed. All these people were doing something co-ordinated and they wondered, all of a sudden, 'What's going on here?'

Now they went around with their heads held high. They had an organising committee. The wins started to come. Management started trying to solve small issues here there and everywhere, including on cleaning chemicals. At that point, the branch went forward with a collective grievance with 200 names on it.

They've now won the big thing they all wanted: the same contracts with contracted hours, up to 35 hours should they wish. That means they don't need three different jobs. One contract, one job. They won paid breaks, proper PPE, proper training. They've got the ability to hold union meetings and stand up. That's the biggest win.

We moved on to a car parking campaign. The car park used to be £20 per month and they were going to move it up to a fiver a day, sometimes a tenner a day. Bizarre, NCP-type charges. Within 24 hours, 370 members signed up to our campaign. That went into a collective grievance. Management opposed it and we said: 'These are the poorest paid workers you're hitting, what cleaner can afford a tenner a day?' That was another victory, because now the cleaners can park for free.

When it started, I would go into the meetings with them. Now they've got the ability to have their meetings and then go into management and tell them what they want. One time, 20 of them turned up. Having the confidence to actually say when something is wrong is a big win. Where they had no reps, they have nine reps. Where they had 30 members, they have 270. Strong.

They themselves had taken on the power, they themselves had taken on the collective grievance. They had taken their issues to management and said: 'We want these solving.' It was awe-inspiring. It started off with cleaners, then it broke out into estates, then further out to technicians and you could see this ripple effect. People realised that when you organise and collectivise, that's what you can achieve.

Time for Inclusive Education

Jordan Daly and Liam Stevenson

In 2014, 19-year-old student and 34-year-old tanker driver – and union rep – Liam met at a foodbank fundraiser. Soon, they were campaigning to make vital changes to the experiences of LGBT school pupils. Their work received significant backing from the union movement.

Jordan: I'm an adult now, but when I was at school, both Primary and Secondary, in common with pretty much every LGBT person I've met, I had a tough experience. When I was going through Primary school, it was the beginning of the 'That's so gay' generation – things that people didn't like were described as being gay, so the message that sent me was that being gay is wrong. Homophobic slurs were always being used as well, openly and without challenge, so it gave the impression that it was OK to do that.

I was nine or ten when I knew I was gay. I remember in Primary 5, I had a crush on a male popstar – Lee from Steps! – but I knew I wasn't going to go back into school and tell anyone. I wonder now how I had that impression that it would be wrong or shameful. It wasn't from parents or teachers; it has to have been the school environment among kids. Every time gay people were spoken about, it was with negative connotations.

Homophobia was never challenged and that continued into secondary school. I started to encounter more direct bullying there. I was grappling with experiencing bullying behaviours and not being sure how to speak up and talk about that – they were targeting me with homophobic slurs, but I didn't dare tell a teacher because I thought they would ask me if I was gay and I didn't know how I'd answer that. At the same time as trying to navigate through avoiding being bullied, I was also trying to navigate coming to terms with being gay and with who I was and accepting that.

That took me on a rapid downward spiral. In my first year of high school, I was suicidal for some time. I had ideas and plans in place for what I was going to do. That followed me through the first few years of high school. Nothing changed for me there. The comments never stopped. There were even incidents with teachers. In my school, two girls got together and held hands. It was a massive scandal. The teachers split them up and their parents were called. I remember thinking: I cannot do this. If people find out that I am gay, it is going to be a nightmare. So I never came out at school. I left when I was 18 and a year later I met Liam.

Liam: One night shortly after we met, over a few glasses of wine Jordan began to tell me about his experiences of growing up as a young gay person in my hometown. He told me where that took him. At that point, I wasn't the most PC person in the world and used all the negative language that forces LGBT people into bad places, I was that guy, I used those slurs, I was a product of that environment and that was the way people like me spoke. If someone was being bullied or harassed for being LGBT, though, I would always be on the side of that person. I realised that my behaviour and thought processes were not aligned with each other. At the same time, I had a three-year-old child, and I realised that her future could not be what Jordan had gone through if she was to grow up and be LGBT. Very quickly we decided we were going to change the world. We didn't know how, we had never been proper campaigners, but we knew we had to.

One of the things I remembered from my education was learning about apartheid South Africa. That helped build compassion, empathy and anti-racism. So we knew it could be done in schools for LGBT issues and we decided on an educational approach to transfer the way we view and treat LGBT young people. We believed that LGBT inclusive education in and across the curriculum in Scotland was the answer. We knew it wouldn't be a silver bullet, and it would take time, maybe even a generation.

Jordan: I watched a documentary, *How To Survive A Plague*, about American activists who advocated for HIV and AIDS awareness during the epidemic. I was in floods of tears watching it, realising there were other people like me, and what they had gone through in this massive culture of homophobia. That was inspirational. I wondered why I had never heard of any of this stuff at school. That was also the moment that I went from being embarrassed and ashamed of being gay to being happy and comfortable. I wish I had learnt about that sooner, and learnt about role models that were like me through history. I learned about suffragettes and the civil rights movement and I looked up to those people, and yet I felt robbed of the fact that LGBT history wasn't being taught or talked about. It felt like a massive injustice and that was the fundamental principle – pupils learning about LGBT history and about prejudice – that Time for Inclusive Education (TIE), our campaign, was founded on. If everyone could be taught these things, we could inspire generations of empathetic and understanding young people.

Liam: We had to go and speak to people and learn about how education and campaigning worked. How could we make these changes? We asked activists how you build a campaign. Someone asked us who was going to fund our campaign – print, travel and all the rest. At first, I used my own money. We hadn't even thought about that.

Jordan: At the start, Liam asked me what would've made school better. I said that learning about people like me, people who had overcome struggle, and hearing that it was OK to be who I was – that was what I was missed. That gives pride and self-confidence. In 2015, when we got started, it didn't feel like much was happening. There was an approach to bullying in schools that did mention homophobic and transphobic bullying, but I knew myself having just left school that nothing was being embedded, and that there wasn't anything in the curriculum about LGBT people, and no robust or strong resources out there. It was all boxed into sex and relationship resources, there was no social aspect, no historical elements. So we decided to set up TIE.

We started a Scottish Parliament petition in June 2015, and over that summer we were introduced to trade unionists who had been involved in different campaigns before, some of whom helped us. We did street stalls, flyered in the city centre, went to Edinburgh with our printed petitions. We gave evidence in the Scottish Parliament to the Public Petitions Committee on that petition, which was terrifying. We spoke our case, we got Committee support and I thought this might be it, we might be straight in, the petition would be advanced.

But in January 2016, we were told that the petition was being closed because they felt at the time they couldn't insert anything into the curriculum. We were angry about it. But that actually spurred us on.

Liam: Following that, people expected us to go away, but that wasn't going to happen. It was a setback, nothing more. We came back with a fresh approach.

Jordan: 2016 was when the trade unions started getting more involved. Liam was a tanker driver and a union rep. He explained the case to the Unite Petroleum Branch at Grangemouth and they were the first to support us financially, with a £500 donation.

Liam: With that we printed a booklet about LGBT people's experiences and sent a copy to every MSP. We made the campaign emotive and shared these awful experiences. The trade unions then really started to pay attention to us too.

Jordan: We'd gained a lot of media attraction and support. Then Unison became the first trade union to forward a motion to officially back the campaign. I was asked to give a speech at their conference – with my baseball cap on backwards, my tattoos out; someone suggested that I was like someone out of a boyband – and I did that off the cuff. I can't really remember it but it was passionate and I was very aware that getting a big union like Unison on board was a big deal. That was the first standing ovation I ever got in my life.

Liam: It lasted five minutes. It was electrifying. The top table immediately agreed to sign a cheque for £1,000 in support of the campaign. We then started getting the support of other trade unions, and the STUC backed us and that was a huge moment. We felt the power of that.

Jordan: I remember being so nervous about that – this is the STUC! If they endorse us, this is the Scottish trade union movement. The motion passed and I remember thinking what a huge moment that was. It also meant that the education unions were involved, and soon the EIS affiliated to TIE. That was incredible. We had also been in and out of parliament, talking to MSPs, and building support there. Political parties were passing motions of support and getting on board.

So much happened in 2016, and 2017 was the year all of that had been building towards. That year we started the TIE Pledge – five key asks of things like curriculum inclusion, LGBT history, teacher training – and we took that to the Parliament to try and get MSPs to sign it. It also committed them to voting for legislation in this area if required.

Liam: This pledge wasn't just a photo opportunity; it was a call to action.

Jordan: There was a core group of six MSPs that had already signed up but we wanted to get a majority of MSPs to sign up, so more than 63, by the end of February, which is LGBT History Month. The campaigners we told about this plan thought that was impossible.

We put so much into that. We were in Edinburgh so often, Liam on his days off from work and me missing lectures at university. And we got it. It took seven weeks, but we got it before the end of February. A majority in the chamber had supported LGBT inclusive education.

Liam: The minute we got a majority for the Pledge, it was a game-changer and the Scottish Government had to do something. We requested a short-life Working Group, with every stakeholder in education around the table, for all types of school. While we'd been campaigning, we'd also been researching how everything could work. We wanted to stay involved and be on that Working Group, and not just leave it to others.

It concluded in 18 months, and it made 33 recommendations to Scottish ministers. We were told to expect that they would try and water them down and back pedal, but the recommendations came back to us and they hadn't asked to have one comma amended. They accepted all 33. We had got everything we had asked for. It was a huge moment.

At the last Parliament sitting before the Summer recess in 2018, we wanted to make a visual statement. There was an idea from the Labour MSP, Daniel Johnson, that we should give all supportive MSPs ties, physical replicas of our logo. We wanted to source the work of making these ties locally, so it would cost £1,000, which we didn't have. The trade unions gave us the money for that.

Then, the Presiding Officer tried to ban this and put a circular around saying it wasn't allowed because it was campaigning within the chamber. But a majority of parliament, our supporters, wore them. Some of the women MSPs were resourceful, wearing them around their heads or making them into flowery brooches.

Jordan: It was such a significant moment. All that support. Wow. It was on the news that evening, and I remember thinking: if I was 12 years old, and saw that on the TV, politicians taking a stand and supporting young LGBT people, that would have been amazing for me.

While we have been campaigning, for the last three or four years we have also been delivering services in schools – teacher training, curriculum resources, workshops with pupils where we explore prejudice – and that's now our main focus. Since the beginning of January 2021 we are fully-funded, so this is now what we do. But I'll not be happy enough to leave this work until we see change. We are focused on service delivery and helping schools implement these changes in a way that will tackle prejudice with an educational approach.

Liam: We know already from our data that the work we've been doing has had a positive impact on young people, and now as this work is about to be rolled out nationally, we know that we are taking the first steps of changing the experiences of a whole generation of young people through education. Once you've changed that, you've changed what comes after them.

Jordan: I'm fully aware that somewhere in some schools there are still going to be young people in the position I was in 14 years ago. Until that stops, TIE will be here.

Menopause policy for railway workers

Kim Gibson

A train conductor based in Inverness, Kim is also RMT Branch Secretary for Inverness and the North. Recently, personal experience set her on a path to pushing for a policy change by her employer, ScotRail, that will help many women for years to come.

YOU COULDN'T GET a job on the railway unless you joined the union when I started in 1985. You signed your union papers before you got your contract. You had no choice. I was 18 then, and it took me five or six years to get involved – it's often your first incident, the first thing that goes wrong for you, that prompts you. You look for the rep because you're in a spot of bother and it piques your interest.

I started my menopause early, when I was 43 or 44. I had a horrific time medically at the beginning. When you're walking through trains it is a bit embarrassing. Passengers don't like overheated carriages, but you imagine working when you're menopausal and you've got the heat sweats. It's an absolute nightmare. You have to change your shirt every half an hour because you're soaked. I did eventually take it to my manager and say 'I can't do this until it passes' and he said 'Tough.' It is pretty much like everything else: when something happens to you and there are no answers, you've got to make sure there are answers for the younger people coming up behind you. There were quite a few younger women coming up behind me, and I wanted something in place for them.

In 2016, I sent an email to the Managing Director at the time, Phil Verster. I laid everything out – how many times I'd had to go into the office, and they'd threatened me with disciplinary stages and absence management procedures. I thought, 'Well I've done nothing wrong, so I'm not accepting any of this.' I just got fed up. I went to him and to my surprise he came back and said he understood. His wife had had breast cancer and had an early onset menopause, and he knew exactly what I was talking about. He said he would get it done. Unfortunately, a year later, he left the job.

We got new management in and it kind of got dropped. I brought it up again and again and again. I went back to them and said, 'This has been promised, where is it?' There was always something else coming up. All of these things cost money to implement and change and there are other things they want to spend the money on. I get that.

It was a bit frustrating. I did some talks at STUC conferences and what have you and there we were telling people how to go about getting a menopause policy in their workplaces. And they had their policies in place before I did. I felt such a fraud.

We tried other things. We challenged the absence monitoring side of things through me. Anything that I was off with, I would give my reason as the menopause, just to see if these managers would put me onto further disciplinary stages. It was a risk, but sometimes you have to put your head on the block. They would put me onto the stages, I would challenge it, and it would get taken back down again. We had to keep challenging things.

My own manager became very well versed in the menopause. I made it my business to go around every GP surgery and pick up every leaflet and booklet associated with the menopause and made sure he had it. It was a running joke – I'd ask him a question from a pamphlet I'd given him and he'd have to give me the right answer or I got an extra three hours off. I never got any three hours off!

We started up an RMT Scotland Women's Group, which now has 200 plus members. That group launched a survey about sexual harassment in the workplace in early 2018. We were gobsmacked at the number of blokes that came forward. It made me think, 'I'm going to see if I can get some of the men to go on record for me about this menopause policy.' I spoke to some of the older men in lots of different depots that I worked at. We'd have full on conversations about this in the mess rooms. They told me stories about how they were coming into work knackered because their wives were not sleeping well because of the heat and the sweats, or they just couldn't sleep at all because they couldn't clear their heads.

When I showed the management this information, I don't know if it kick-started it, or they suddenly thought 'Hang on a minute, this really is a problem in the workplace.' These people I was talking to were drivers or signallers or other safety critical members of staff, and although these blokes were not going through it, their wives were, and that meant they were going through fatigue. The railway is still a male-dominated industry, though nowhere near what it was when I started, and so showing that men were affected too got things moving, or made them rethink it anyway.

I wanted a policy so that any worker could go to any manager and say to them, 'I'm really struggling, this is what's happening' and that manager would understand. Even if they didn't like it, they knew they had to handle it and handle it well and sensitively. That's all I really wanted. That kind of comfort.

Eventually, in 2019, we got a menopause policy that did that and I couldn't be happier about that. It has a policy number and that makes it difficult to take away without replacing it with something better. They now do things like distribute handheld fans to all members of staff so that menopausal women aren't singled out. They put on little roadshows and the Menopause Café. They are doing those things that now mean you can talk about it in comfort.

I set the ball rolling, but everybody that contributed to the conversations we had got this policy across the line. A number of wonderful women from my union and others were also instrumental – Fiona Steele and Annette Drylie to name two. The STUC gave me a platform to talk about this at Congress, and made sure I had people to talk to, and gave me a lot of support.

I think that's the role of older trade union women: we've got to do the deed and put our heads on the block to make it easier for younger women coming through. We've also got to show them that if they want something done, they can stand up for themselves.

Bargaining for NHS workers

Lilian Macer

Though picket lines grab attention, most vital trade union work is undertaken behind the scenes. It involves engaging with the nitty-gritty of policy to make long-term gains for members, as exemplified by Lilian's account of NHS Agenda for Change negotiations.

WITH MY DAD being a miner, I was always aware of unions and joined one when I started working. But my activism started in 1999 when the government announced their PFI scheme for NHS Lanarkshire. I was a cook in a hospital and domestic staff like me were going to be transferred over to the private sector.

Around that time, the Agenda for Change programme was announced. Its aim was to bring in a new grading and pay system for NHS staff, one that would streamline pay scales across different sectors of the health service. Up until then, it was all different – we had one employer but different conditions for each type of worker group. If you were in nursing and midwifery for example, you got additional holiday entitlement; if you were ancillary, which as a cook I was, and also the porters were, then terms and conditions were not as favourable. How you were treated depended on which section you were in.

There were also two pay structures. Nursing and midwifery had a pay review body, others had pay bargaining. Effectively within the NHS you had different pay systems, different terms and conditions and everyone was treated differently within that one employer. There was a real pressure around equal pay, a real drive to ensure that we had an equality-proof system put in place and Agenda For Change gave the opportunity to create and develop and deliver that equality-proofed job evaluation system across the whole workforce.

Negotiations were complex and ran for a long time. There were numerous steering groups and working groups, but a lot of it was shrouded in secrecy. Through the negotiations, there were highs and lows, and things that were tabled that didn't find their way into the final outcome.

However, there was a group established to look at the job evaluation system itself and to look at the job profiles – what all the jobs were, who did what, who was paid what. Within a relatively short time – a couple of years – the group developed 500 national profiles which looked at every job within the NHS across the UK. Then the unions went out to engage with union branches. After that, we started to look at some of the concerns that were raised.

Back around the negotiating table, we pushed to get additional profiles and revised profiles and also to revise the scheme itself. There was a huge amount of work undertaken, and every trade union was involved to some degree.

One of the major issues for us was around the skills, knowledge and development of the workforce. We developed a knowledge and skills framework. We referred to that as 'the good part' of Agenda for Change. That really put training and development on the map for those who didn't necessarily get access to it in the past. Every worker now had the right to access learning, training and development through the framework.

Once there was wider engagement with reps on the ground, we again quickly realised that it wasn't just the job evaluation scheme, but the terms and conditions that needed a lot of work. One of the sticking points was around unsocial hours and on-call payments These were completely different from area to area. The new arrangements looked to harmonise these, but they seemed to harmonise down.

If you were an ancillary worker you would get time and a half on a Saturday, and double time on a Sunday. These new arrangements looked to mirror nursing and midwifery, which was time and a third and time and two thirds respectively. That meant a huge pay cut for ancillary workers. This was not sustainable; it was seriously disadvantageous to the lowest paid in our workplace. We needed to do something about it. As a compromise, they unpicked the unsocial hours, and took them out of the agreement.

We eventually settled on a scheme of tapered unsocial hours, which worked better. In October 2004, all of the trade unions bar one accepted and agreed the new arrangements. Agenda for Change was implemented.

There was a huge sigh of relief, but a realisation of the huge job needed now to implement it all. We didn't have huge amounts of reps trained in job evaluation, and this new system meant that we needed to have as many reps trained as possible. The panels that looked at every job in your health board consisted of two reps from the trade unions and two people from NHS management. So it was a huge job of training the trainers, which we did as a partnership between unions and management. My job from 2004 to 2009 was helping to develop those panels. The partnership approach was fantastic, and the integrity of the process was maintained. Not everyone was happy with the outcome of their post and moved to the appeals process.

There have been a number of positives from Agenda for Change. The relationships between the NHS employers and the unions improved and partnership working became embedded, building awareness that we needed an equality-proof system in every NHS board in Scotland. We now have a bank of experienced job evaluators. They can evaluate, they can do job analysis, they can write accurate job descriptions. That was all done through the training programme we had. That expertise now exists.

The jobs within the NHS have developed way beyond 2004 when they were originally evaluated; staff have taken on extended roles with additional responsibilities which require increased knowledge, training and experience. We need to make sure that there are constant monitoring arrangements in place, ensuring posts are re-evaluated so that staff are paid at the appropriate grade for the role they do. Therefore, the maintenance of Agenda for Change is critical if we are to ensure the equality-proofed system still exists within the NHS.

Keeping guards on trains

Mary Jane Herbison

Mary Jane became an assistant ticket examiner for a few months in the 1990s. Twenty-five years later, she remains on the railway as a conductor and RMT rep. In 2016, she was part of the campaign to keep guards on the newly-electrified line between Edinburgh and Glasgow.

I ALWAYS KNEW about trade unions. My dad was a fitter in the Caledonian Works in Springburn and mum was a union member too. That was in the days of Thatcher, and I remember my dad going out on strike because the nurses were out and I asked why. He said 'It's just what you do, it's solidarity.'

There had been talk for years about the electrification of the line and they were gonna bring the faster trains in. As soon as they want to electrify trains, driver-only becomes the buzzword, because that's what's happened everywhere. They get rid of the guards. So the alarm bells were ringing.

The electric trains were coming in on the Glasgow to Edinburgh line. The investment had been made, they were putting up the stanchions. Union branches like mine put resolutions to RMT head office saying 'we need to be ready for this fight' – we know they are coming for the conductors and want these trains to be driver-only. Abellio – the train operating company – will say it's more efficient and will run faster. They will demote conductors to ticket examiners, and trains can leave without ticket examiners.

There was a safety aspect too. We felt having a trained safety-critical member of staff on a train makes it safer for passengers, and the public like to see that presence in the carriage so that if anything goes wrong, they know there is a second person there.

We started with mass meetings and we began to speak about

balloting for strike action as we knew that was the only way we could get the company to listen to us. The Scottish Government got involved as well, saying 'It's not really up to us, it's an industrial matter.' But ultimately it was Transport Scotland and the Government that were saying they wanted the trains to be driver-only. They said it made the trains go faster because it reduced dwelling time at stations. With a conductor, he or she makes sure the train is on the platform properly, opens the doors and steps off to check things are OK. They were saying that extra time was costing time and money.

We made the point that a quicker journey isn't a safer one and that a second, fully-trained person was important if anything happened. We have to keep proving our training all the time – we are tested every two years with over 300 questions, we have to know the route we're on so if the train comes off the line we know exactly where we are. We kept highlighting that we were heavily trained; we don't just sell tickets.

They kept coming back to the line that it was just about who opens and closes doors, and we had to say it's not, there's much more to our role. That's what the company said and what the media picked up because they always take that side. We kept saying again and again, this is all about safety. No-one was looking for a pay rise, after all.

The public understood that and supported us. On 11 days of picket lines, we never had anyone coming up and opposing us, which was unique. There was support from other unions too – some ASLEF members joined the RMT so they wouldn't have to cross picket lines, there was support from GMB and USDAW who would come and bring coffee. They could see why we were striking.

It all worked, because we got a victory. It was probably a combination of reasons. We'd had 11 days on strike and the Edinburgh Festival was about to start – August is incredibly busy on that line, day and night, and we were about to call more strike days. Queen Street station had been electrified, the station had reopened, and they knew we were going to go on strike. Eventually, the Scottish Government got involved – they can when it suits them! – and basically said to Abellio: give them what they want, or something here, because we can't have the festivals disrupted and the station is reopening.

We ended up with a compromise that the drivers opened the doors and we closed them. So that guaranteed the role of keeping a guard on the train and kept the safety aspect going – even when the drivers were opening doors, we were there to hop onto the platform and check the train was on the platform safely. We kept control of the dispatch of the train, which is the most important part – making sure no-one is running up to the train and getting caught in the doors, or falling under the train. If we're not there to spot that, it can be fatal.

We showed that by fighting, you can win. We kept the guards on the train.

Saving the Fife yards

Michael Sullivan

Michael joined the boilermakers of the Methil Oil and Gas Yard in 1972. He became active in the union, building on the proud Fife traditions he had grown up with. Almost a half century later, he was key in battles to save local steel fabrication yards, by now making parts for the renewable energy sector.

IN 2001 THE Methil yard closed, which was a disgrace as there was a chance to keep it open and we never took it. Lots of other big yards closed too. There was now a gap in the market for small offshore work and from 2001 a new firm called BiFab – Burntisland Fabrication – went after all of these projects. Slowly but surely they progressed and moved onto some bigger projects in the North Sea. They reopened the Arnish, Burntisland and Methil yards. They relied heavily on the old oil and gas workforce to do the work for them, and that workforce was the jewel in their crown.

I joined BiFab in 2003 after being laid off in 2001 following many years of service at Methil. It was a chance to get back working in that yard. They were very anti-union at that time, but clients who are putting major structures into the North Sea want to know how companies will handle their workforce – health and safety and how they will communicate with them. BiFab preferred a works committee, but that wasn't the same as a union structure.

Eventually, around 2006, I started to get involved – I didn't do it early on because if BiFab thought you were going to be a problem, they would just pay you off. They were a hire and fire company. It was that kind of fear and atmosphere that we were working with for the first five years. But once the union did come in, it settled down a bit. They weren't paying the union rate, and that was the first dispute we had. We asked for that, we went out for almost six weeks on an indefinite strike – unusual this century – and that's when the BiFab management realised they'd have to pay those rates and work with the union. When we got that, we said to them that we would work with them to win orders.

They started to work with us, though there was always a sense they resented that, and more disputes followed. They started using more agency workers and not extending the full-time staff, because agency workers were easy to get rid of. We had to get the same conditions for agency workers as we full-time workers had. We never discriminated between the two. The company always said no, but we continued to allow agency workers to union meetings and let them vote on pay even though in the end their votes weren't allowed to be counted. There was no difference to us – a working man is a working man. That helped the workforce when it came to the Battle for BiFab – we were together, a solid unit.

We learned how to go to MPs, MSPs and councillors and meet with different groups and see how they worked and how they could help us. The company saw that we were doing their work for them in trying to win orders. We would lobby to win big contracts for North Sea wind turbine orders.

The first big order where that relationship went wrong was the Beatrice order, which would see us supply wind turbine jacket substructures for the Beatrice offshore wind farm. By that time, BiFab were running out of clients to work with. Their attitude to clients was terrible, as was their attitude to politicians. People that tried to help them, they dismissed. They wanted to do everything themselves. We had to say, 'We're not doing Beatrice for BiFab, we're doing it for the three yards we've got. We're doing it for the workforce.' A lot of workers and others like politicians resented BiFab. Because we said that this was for the workers and not BiFab, and we lobbied at Holyrood and Westminster and ran a campaign, they managed to get an order of 33 of these jackets.

The BiFab relationship with the client on that job deteriorated, and BiFab were not going to get any more work. It was only when we upped our campaigns and lobbying that work would come in. There was another successful example of that with an order from Premier Oil to make Solan jackets. There should have been a follow-up order, but they just wouldn't work with BiFab management.

All of this built up to the Battle for BiFab. After Premier Oil, a new client had come in, Seaway Heavy Lifting. They were as ruthless as BiFab, so it was toxic from the start. You could see from the start of the project that something wasn't right between the clients and BiFab. Eventually, Seaway had enough and said they weren't going to pay anymore and were going to take the work somewhere else.

At that point, I was in a meeting with Human Resources and the BiFab managing director came in and told me that they were going into administration, and asked me what my opinion was. I told him that nothing would be moving out of our three yards. We would take control of them and not allow anything to be taken out. He told me they had 10 days until administration, but the yard was now in our hands. Then he walked out. He had tears in his eyes, he was genuine, but they could see no other way out. They had no money.

We in the union sat down and it took a while to grasp the situation. The men had left for the weekend by then, and over that weekend we decided that instead of occupying the yards, we'd have a work-in. Nothing would come in or move out – nothing, not even a letter from the postman. We'd stop everything, but we'd work and keep working because that's what we'd done with every other contract. The workforce bought into that. We had such unity at that time. It was a huge week. The GMB came up with the slogan 'Battle for BiFab' and the only regret I have is that we weren't battling for BiFab, we were battling for the workers, so I wished the slogan could've reflected that.

The men did brilliantly. There was not a bit of bother on the sites. They worked and they kept producing. They let nothing in or out of the yards. We got a lot of help from full-time GMB and Unite officials, they worked tirelessly. The GMB and the STUC came up with a plan to have some of the men march down the Royal Mile to Parliament in their overalls.

The first week of the campaign was fantastic. We got so many people on board. Politicians flooded us with support. The community came with us. The march on that Thursday made the campaign. It couldn't be ignored. The First Minister set up a meeting with Seaway and BiFab and right away they thrashed out a deal that enabled us to finish the contract.

The initial impact of marching down the street had worked, but the serious work to try and get other orders into the yards after that contract finished was just beginning. It was then that people started to realise that BiFab was no longer a company you could put work into. We started to campaign nationally and took it to UK ministers and shadow ministers. They started to write letters to companies.

There was a meeting at the end of the Battle for BiFab campaign in St Andrew's House. By that time we had managed to get the Scottish Government to sit down with the unions, the clients, the developers and we all met and it was crystal clear after that meeting that BiFab was no longer a viable company to put work into. We came out of that meeting knowing that BiFab were not going to win any contracts, and we were going to have to change dramatically.

That's when we decided to start the Fife – Ready for Renewal campaign. That was about going to the community and getting them on our side, and all the different groups too. We'd been told in that meeting in St Andrew's House that EDF, the big electrical company, were about to put this order for a lot of jackets to Indonesia and transport them halfway around the world and put them five miles outside our yard. We said, 'We can't allow that to happen.' And it did happen. They put the contracts to Indonesia. The Fife – Ready for Renewal campaign aimed to highlight that – they would rather build these things halfway around the world than give them to BiFab. That shows you how toxic the BiFab name was. We couldn't hide that anymore.

The community and all the groups that came with us were fantastic. It was different to the Beatrice campaign and the Battle for BiFab which were mainly about lobbying politicians. With Fife – Ready for Renewal, we targeted EDF. We had a meeting at Buckhaven. We left an empty seat because we asked them to come and talk to the community and tell them why they were building these jackets 35,000 miles away, and they didn't come. We saw at that meeting that we had the backing of the whole community and we decided we'd go to the EDF offices in Edinburgh. They panicked when they saw us all outside there. Dave Moxham of the STUC was brilliant. He organised that.

We told them we would go national with our campaign. We said, 'We've got the community on our side, we'll stop paying our electricity bills.' We said nobody in Fife will go with EDF now. People in communities put on pressure, they raised the ethical and environmental issues too. Finally, EDF turned around and said that if the campaign stopped, they'd commission eight jackets from the Methil yard.

From Polaris to a Scottish Parliament

Pat Milligan

Pat has been a trade unionist for over 60 years. As a rep and branch secretary in various workplaces, and then an STUC employee, she has played a part in many campaigns during that time. Here she recounts a few highlights, including the drive for a Scottish Parliament.

IN THE MID-1960s, uncles of mine used to visit the family home. One of them was very much into unions and another would go more on what the priest told him. So I was aware of these different arguments. I came from a big family, and my dad worked in the shipyards. I used to wonder who was going to help poorer people like us, and it wasn't going to be an abstract God or the wee priest down the road. Later on, during things like the miners' strike, the trade union people always made more sense to me than the parish priest. I respect people who rely on it and believe in it, but religion wasn't for me. I like the trade union way of trying to balance the books and make life better for everyone.

I started working in the late 1950s, but more than anything it was when the Polaris submarine base came to Dunoon in 1961 that I became involved. I then mixed more with people who were trade unionists as well as peace activists. I was always a union member and then a branch secretary from then on, and in those years a member of the Communist Party of Great Britain too.

I actually got jailed protesting at Polaris. All the women were put in one big cell and the men in another. We were singing songs like 'You cannae spend a dollar when you're deid.' I was young and I thought it was wonderful. Then one by one the other women were taken and charged. I was the last one in the cell and I started crying! We didn't have a phone in our house and the local fuzz from our police station had to go and tell my parents that I was in a cell in Dunoon. My mum was raging at me. 'You're a constant source of embarrassment' she said to me at one point. My brothers loved that.

At the outset of the early campaigns for a Scottish Parliament, I wasn't convinced. I was thinking more about internationalism. But I changed my way of thinking. Thatcher played a big part in that, the way she was, what she did to the miners.

By the 1990s, there was a lot of momentum for a Scottish Parliament. I felt that Scotland could be a better nation with a parliament, and it would care about the rest of the world. I thought we could set a better example. And also, you're closer to home – you can put pressure more easily on politicians who aren't doing what you're asking of them, whereas Westminster is so distant.

Donald Dewar was our MP at that point, and I knew him quite well as my mum and her friend – they called them Cagney and Lacey! – they were on the committee of the local social club. They had a 200 Club Dance every year and Donald used to come to it. I also met him through other campaigns and work, for instance when I was doing some jobs for the CND. I liked him very much. I remember talking to him a lot about it all, and I liked how he explained the case for a Scottish Parliament. And he thought my mum was great.

The campaign kept going and I was involved, again with note-taking, this time for the Scottish Constitutional Convention's meetings. When the result was announced and we knew there was going to be a parliament, it was a fantastic moment. The STUC was crucial in the campaign for the parliament. It struck me when I was taking minutes in those meetings the many different people that were there. The STUC brought them together. It was a uniting force. I think it was the making of the campaign.

Saving school kitchens

Paul Arkison

Organisers like Paul provide a crucial link between unions and workers. They help co-ordinate campaigns and unleash the potential of members to force changes and resist cuts. The successful 2014 drive to save school kitchens in South Ayrshire is a perfect example.

MY DAD'S BACKGROUND was in the shipyards. He told me about when he was an apprentice and the shipyard tried to take away the welders' free daily bottle of milk. The milk was supposed to stop their throats and insides getting covered with dust. My dad and his colleagues fought to keep the milk for everyone, including the apprentices. That story gave me an interest in trade unionism.

A lot of our GMB members are in facilities management – school janitorial, catering, cleansing work. They are predominantly women and predominantly part-time workers. They are very supportive of the union and very readily join in with campaigns. Our local reps are very active too – it makes local councils very nervous when workers who know the job are there in meetings.

Every year there are a series of budget discussions, which really means cuts to services. That year, 2013/14, they proposed that nearly every primary school kitchen in South Ayrshire would close. The larger ones would stay open and the cooking would be done there and in six or seven academy schools. The rest of the kitchens would only be open for serving food. This had a catastrophic impact on our membership. Our membership at South Ayrshire Council was 400; almost 50 per cent of them had some link with a school or a school kitchen.

These proposals were firmed up when the new year began and we went on the rampage. We exposed them for what they were. We started going around all the schools to get people active. We started to get parents active. We started a petition which was called Save Our Schools (SOS). That gathered 2,000 signatures through members attending gala days and taking stalls at events like local firework displays.

It progressed us into new areas. We came into contact with other groups who were campaigning for similar things. If there was a single school in an area, the parents would get together to save their kitchen, and we would join with them and we would assist them and they would assist us.

I visited the schools regularly before the campaign and while it was running. There were some schools where the kitchen staff knew which kids weren't getting a meal at night-time and knew the kids that were coming to school without any breakfast. That was another thing that was going to be lost through the closures.

One school that sticks in my mind was Tarbolton Primary. Its kitchen was identified for closure. That school is the heart and soul of the area. When I visited, the janitor was refereeing a football match, and the catering staff were bringing out sandwiches and juice for the kids. That little moment showed what a part of the community it was. The whole village got behind the campaign there. There was a village hall meeting there one night when it was clear we were going to win. Local politicians, who at the start had run a million miles from this were going to be there as well. But when the time came, the people of the village wouldn't let them in! They recognised that it was the union that saved the kitchen and they didn't want to hear from the people who had ignored them initially. They only came along when they smelt victory.

The campaign was led up front by the union, but the foundations all came from the membership. They signed the petition, took it around, visited the gala days, got people along. It grew from them. We gave ourselves targets; things like every month we'd aim to have an article in the press about the campaign, or every week we'd visit a certain amount of schools.

There were then a set of fiery meetings because the council detested what we were doing. We presented our petition to a full council meeting. We made it into a theatrical event. It was packed out that day – union members were there, parents were there, newspapers and others. There was a motion by one councillor to overturn the closure proposal. That was voted down because of the numbers and the politics of the council, but the damage that we had done meant the original proposals were overturned and we could begin proper negotiations.

We reached an agreement over the fact that the council needed to shut down some kitchens as they were in such poor conditions – we accepted that as we didn't want our members working in those kitchens. There were 19 kitchens due to close originally, and we got that down to five. The five that were closing were not places you would want anyone to work in. The irony – and the final victory in a way – is that some of the kitchens that did close are now refurbished and reopened.

That campaign shows how you strike fear into big organisations – through workers banding together with the backing of their union.

Saving skilled jobs in a pandemic

Paul Leckie

Paul joined a union aged 15. Forty years later, he was a Unite convenor at the Alexander Dennis bus factory in Falkirk when the Covid-19 pandemic struck. Here he details how union members adapted to circumstances and fought to preserve their jobs.

AT THE BEGINNING of February 2020, I was speaking to the company to get something in the region of 40 temporary workers into Alexander's Falkirk because the order book was going in the right direction. Then the pandemic hit in March. Suddenly we were onto furlough and orders were dropping off a cliff. So in one month we went from talking about extra labour to putting people onto furlough. No-one could be prepared for that.

Normally to get information to the workers, we'd call a factory meeting and I'd stand with a microphone and let everybody know what was happening. Suddenly they were all at home and we didn't have that. That brought its own difficulties and we had to look at other ways to communicate. We set up a website, but it was clear orders weren't coming. We were in serious difficulties.

That's when we started campaigning. We reached out to the members, both Unite and GMB, to ask them to start emailing their MPs and MSPs. The collective effort got us into the door with the Scottish Government and we started talking to them about different ways they might be able to help.

That led to the Scottish Ultra Low Emission Bus Scheme (SULEBS), which funded the building of green-friendly buses. We managed to secure a deal as part of that, and the Scottish Government underwrote a contract with Lothian Buses which kept us ticking over. The SULEBS scheme runs over five years and overall Alexander Dennis won something like 228 vehicles over the first two rounds, so that was a massive help to us, although it didn't quite get us back to where we were. But there was light at the end of the tunnel. It saved skilled jobs.

We used the green angle as well, especially with COP26 coming up. We contacted politicians again and they were receptive, across the parties. As well as SULEBS, there was also a promised 4,000 vehicles from Boris Johnson about a year previously that hadn't come to fruition. So we were trying to push to win some of that funding too.

We hoped and knew the pandemic wasn't going to last forever, and green buses were an opportunity for us to keep jobs, and for operators and politicians from an environmental point of view. They had their targets to meet.

When you're in the position we were in, you leave no stone unturned. I gave a spiel to the Friends of the Earth at one of their conferences on Zoom. I spoke with Falkirk councillors to get them on board. We kept up the emails and trying to speak with politicians, but we were also conscious that it wasn't just our industry looking for help. We didn't want to get lost in the mire. Every sector was trying, we had to keep ourselves at the forefront and the green angle helped with that. The tactic was to keep it as high profile as possible and keep up the pressure.

That was a collective effort from us up here and from the guys at the Alexander factory in Scarborough. The members in Falkirk and Scarborough played their part with the emails to MPs. One of the members here in fact went and chapped on his MP's door because he lived close by and asked him why he hadn't replied to his email. But it worked, because he engaged with us quite often after that!

There were job losses, but we at least battled and managed to avoid compulsory redundancies. We used furlough to keep kicking the ball as far away down the park as we could. We made it so that nobody *had* to leave. It was sad that we lost jobs, but the losses were voluntary and among guys who'd reached a certain age and were happy to go.

You always see the benefits of a collective voice. Everyone pulling in the same direction, that gets you through.

Blind workers' rights

Robert Mooney

Robert has been a union member since beginning work at Blindcraft in 1979. As well as being a shop steward, he served on the STUC General Council for 17 years and the STUC Disability Committee. Here, he gives an account of trade union gains for blind and disabled workers.

I WENT TO a school for the partially sighted and left there in 1971. That was the first year that kids from 'special needs' schools could sit their O-Levels, which is shocking. If you had a disability, you weren't allowed to get the qualifications. That's not that long ago. So I left school without any qualifications, and any education I got was through the trade union movement. It turned my life around. It gave me a lot of opportunities that I would never have had if I'd not join the union.

I learnt about the history of blind activism too. Back in 1920 there was a Blindness March, run by the National League of the Blind. Blind people from all over the country – including Scotland – marched to London and had a demonstration about their rights. Eventually their campaign resulted in the Blindness Act of 1926, the first act for disability that went through parliament. It was the first march of its kind, and it was replicated throughout the trade union movement after that. The Jarrow March was based on what the blind did in 1920.

I joined the Glasgow Blindcraft factory – called Royal Strathclyde Blind Craft Industries now – in 1979. Blindcraft has an enormous history in Glasgow. It has been here since 1904 on different sites. It employed blind and partially sighted people up until the late 1960s, and then they opened it up to people with other disabilities. In the 1940s and 50s, they employed about 550 blind people. They had

100 sewing machines. This is anecdotal, but when I became a shop steward and talked to some of the existing reps there, they always said that Blindcraft was one of the first, if not the first, to provide equal pay for women in the city.

Back when I joined we made beds and office furniture. We were run by the social work department which was the wrong place to be as social workers don't have a great insight into business. We really struggled until 1997. We had a turnover of £3 million and we were losing £2 million a year. Then, City Building took over the running of it. They turned it round within 18 months. We went to a £29 million turnover and were making money.

We weren't paid an awful lot when I joined. Conditions have moved on enormously. That started when City took over, but it was a joint effort with the trade unions. Management couldn't have done it without the support of the trade unions. There had been unfair practices – some people on the shop floor in 1997 who were getting £80 bonus a week, but there was others getting nothing, or £5. Within a year, we negotiated that everyone would get a set bonus of £47. After a while we got that up to £80 and *then* we managed to get it consolidated into our pay, so it became part of our pension.

There's 360 people working there now, 180 of them have disabilities. It's real jobs with good conditions and half-decent pay. At the moment we furnish all the homeless accommodation in Glasgow. We have ten teams of three people going out and furnishing houses every day. All the products are made in the factory, including the duvet covers, pillowcases, curtains, three-piece suites and dining tables, everything. They put the floors down. We make office furniture and fit it for some of the biggest offices in Glasgow. We make frames for timber kit houses too.

Today, and it's not a massive amount of money by any means, but the lowest paid disabled person in there gets £22,000 a year, which is a good bit above the living wage, and good holidays, for a 36-hour week. That was all through the efforts of the trade unions.

Battle for Royal Mail

Tam Dewar

Tam has been a union member all his working life, including during a stint as an ice cream man. In the 1990s he became a postal worker and has taken part in a number of successful actions to protect conditions, culminating in the 2018 battle to save Royal Mail.

I'VE ALWAYS BEEN aware that I'm a member of the working class and that members of the working class need to join a union to defend their rights and represent themselves against employers, who have the real power. I've had that realisation since I was 16. My English teacher at school was Willie McIlvanney and he took us through a play called *Willie Rough* about Red Clydeside.

When I joined Royal Mail it was a public service. Posties started at 5.30am, sorted the mail, left the office at 7am and delivered all the mail before 10am. Then we went back into the office, sorted the mail that had come in while we were out and delivered the rest of it for 1pm. The public got the best service in the world – two postal deliveries in a day. We had to fight to defend that.

Unfortunately, the New Labour government brought a couple of spivs in – Allan Leighton and Adam Crozier – to run Royal Mail and they brought in a single daily delivery. It was based on the supermarket policy of 'just in time', which is not really suited to an efficient postal service. So we had to fight that from the start, and to fight privatisation. And we had to fight them from shutting the final salary pension scheme. It's been a constant battle. We now have a better working relationship with Royal Mail.

Privatisations cut staff numbers and costs, and they cut terms and conditions and maximise profits for shareholders. That was the plan for Royal Mail. We had a CEO who wanted first to break up Royal Mail into component parts. That would have put one part of the business in competition with another. You'd be transferred and you would work under the market conditions – zero hours contracts, no annual leave, no sick pay, no pension.

So there was a big fight in 2018 to stop that happening. We campaigned through traditional methods like speaking to people at gate meetings and passing on news through the written word, but social media played a much bigger part in that dispute than any before. Facebook, Twitter, video calls – new tactics to people of my generation.

The union came close to losing the battle, but we held our nerve. Solidarity in the postal industry has always been instrumental to defending our terms and conditions, both inside the business and externally. For example, when the college lecturers who educate our children go on strike, we don't deliver the mail, we don't cross the picket line. When it comes to defending ourselves it's very, very strong. We had a 'yes' vote for action that stretched beyond the 90 per cent mark. Royal Mail knew we were unassailable. Eventually, and never in my experience has this happened, the CEO of a FTSE 100 company – Royal Mail – was forced out by the trade union. The company brought in a CEO that was willing to deal with us. We had defeated this attempt to cut the feet off the postal service and turn us into an Amazon.

No matter where you live in the UK, you will see the red uniform of Royal Mail delivery workers. Everybody receives something through the post. From rural communities to the big cities, a lot of people know their posties personally. We do have a lot of public support – we saw that during Covid when we worked through the first lockdown onwards.

Not only were we fighting Covid, we were fighting the employer. In common with other public sector workers, we had to fight to get PPE. We had to fight to get protective measures at work. We had to fight to get safe distancing. We had to fight to stop the practice of sending two people out in a van. The employer took a couple of weeks to respond, but in Scotland and Northern Ireland we started having meetings on Zoom which meant we could contact workers from Ballymena, Belfast, Aberdeen, Dundee – that allowed us to find out what was happening locally and to put pressure on the business to deliver for workers.

We must have been one of the first major companies to secure PPE and social distancing. We were able to maintain the service, even though some postal workers were understandably hesitant and we suffered with absence and illness as much as anybody.

I'll always be part of a union.

Repealing Section 2A

Tracy Gilbert

In 1988, a law was passed which prevented local authorities from the 'intentional promotion of homosexuality'. Tracy was among many trade unionists and others who joined together to campaign for its repeal, eventually granted by the Scottish Parliament in 2000.

WHEN I WAS 18, I started working at Edinburgh Council and later became a Unison shop steward there. I was involved with, what was then called, the Lesbian and Gay Self-Organisation Group. There were quite a lot of campaigns at the time, and one of them was against Section 2A as it was called in Scotland, and Section 28 elsewhere in the UK. We were heavily involved in the fight to repeal that. We were just one of many voices from across the whole trade union movement.

My partner had two kids who were both at primary school. Section 2A meant that lesbian and gay relationships couldn't be discussed within educational settings, so there could be no mention of any family that wasn't stereotypically one man, one woman and kids. It created additional problems for people working in education if they were lesbian or gay because they felt the legislation made it impossible to come out at work. The Act prevented teachers supporting young people who were gay, and acknowledge that there were children that came from same sex households. This applied across all educational settings and any other local government funded bodies at that time.

It was introduced by Margaret Thatcher to undermine the acceptance of same sex relationships and to end the increasing recognition that it was normal that people could be out and proud.

Brian Souter (millionaire businessman) funded a private referendum and encouraged people to vote against the repeal of the act, and he funded billboards all around us that said same-sex families weren't proper families. I remember a big one on Ferry Road. I was taking the kids to school on the bus and we'd drive past it – this sign saying our family wasn't a real family.

Souter's campaign was vile and vocal. There was a lot opposition from the churches too. The Scottish Parliament hadn't been around long, and this was their first problematic piece of legislation with this run-in with the churches. Wendy Alexander was Social Justice Minister at the time and she was under a lot of pressure from the churches not to support the repeal.

An overarching worry for the general public was that Souter was trying to bankroll this referendum and campaign. People did not want private rich people to be able to buy democracy. So possibly if that hadn't happened, I don't know how far our campaign would've gone. It allowed many people who maybe wouldn't normally be allies to come together and say 'This is wrong. No matter the issue, you shouldn't be able to privately fund the law.' So maybe Souter did us a favour, ironically.

Bill Speirs was head of the STUC at the time. I remember the *Daily Record* doing a spread with the STUC really putting a lot of pressure on working class people to support our community. They published words from Bill and trade union activists saying Section 2A had to go. The *Daily Record* at that point was probably the only daily paper read by the working class and by it publishing pro-lesbian and gay information our campaign reached more ordinary working people. I remember reading it at the time and thinking that this was a pivotal moment – a campaign in the papers that the older generation would read. I felt we could actually defeat Souter and defeat this piece of Thatcher's legislation. That was a crucial turning point, having the working class media with us as well as the trade union movement on our side. Scottish families grew up with that paper and it was not something you expected your dad to be reading about, pro-lesbian and gay rights!

I remember going to various demonstrations outside Holyrood and then later to the House of Commons against Section 28 too. Then the news came that 2A was going. It was so positive that we could create change and change people's lives in this new parliament, and that we could take on big business and the churches and win. To defeat those interests felt big.

We've travelled quite far since then. In terms of LGBT+ rights, we've come much further than we'd ever have dreamed of. We didn't have equal marriage, we didn't have adoption rights, we didn't have insemination rights for fertility. We couldn't serve in the army, donate blood or have next of kin status medically or financially. Age of consent was different. There were all these things that didn't seem like they were going to be possible, things that we've managed to achieve in the last 20+ years. It's been hard fought, but over a relatively short period of time when you think about the history of the trade union movement and the history of lesbian and gay rights within that. I think we've done quite well in terms of driving the agenda forward and creating equality for people.

PART 2

Workers For Change: Portraits

A note on the photographs
Alan McCredie

OF ALL THE many genres available, photographing people has always been my favourite. No portrait session is ever the same and the state of flux that exists between the subject and the photographer is something I am intrigued by. There is a fascination in balancing the need to put people at ease and the requirement to pull something interesting out of the ether.

From factory floor to football training grounds, from Ayrshire to Aberdeen, I have met and photographed some truly special people. Along the way, I spent time with Historic Environment Scotland and Prospect on a walk through the Ochils where every feature of the land was decoded and explained. I had the privilege of a behind-the-scenes tour of the Scottish Mining Museum in Newtongrange with the wonderful ex-NUM man John Kane.

Logistically, the project was not entirely straightforward. Coming out of the worst ravages of the pandemic certainly had an effect in the early months, with many still working from home and several planned photoshoots being postponed due to people catching Covid. But nothing worthwhile is ever easy.

My first portrait was Rab Noakes of the Musicians' Union; my last, some seven or eight months later, was Michael Mackenzie of Equity. Bookended by these stalwarts of Scottish cultural life was as varied a set of people as I have ever had the pleasure to meet.

From a photography point of view, this project celebrating 125 years of the Scottish Trades Union Congress has been solid gold. The strength of the union movement has always been its membership and the diversity it represents. The group of portraits that follow underline, again and again, the power in the unions.

Dan Travis, Broadcasting, Entertainment, Communications and Theatre Union

Jan Usher, Prospect

Abigail Guthrie, Prospect

Ines Lozano, The Workers' Observatory Project

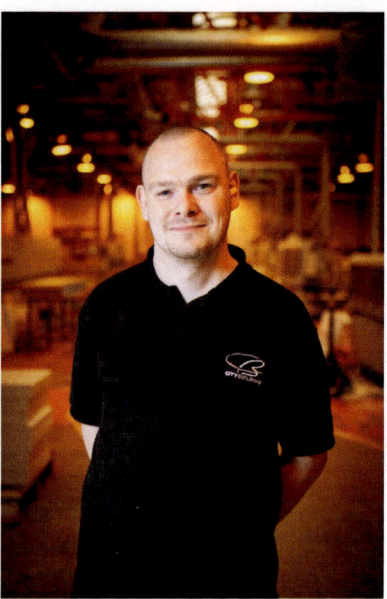

Left: Steven McCluskey, Community
Right: Colin Pellow, Community

Martin McGarvey, Community

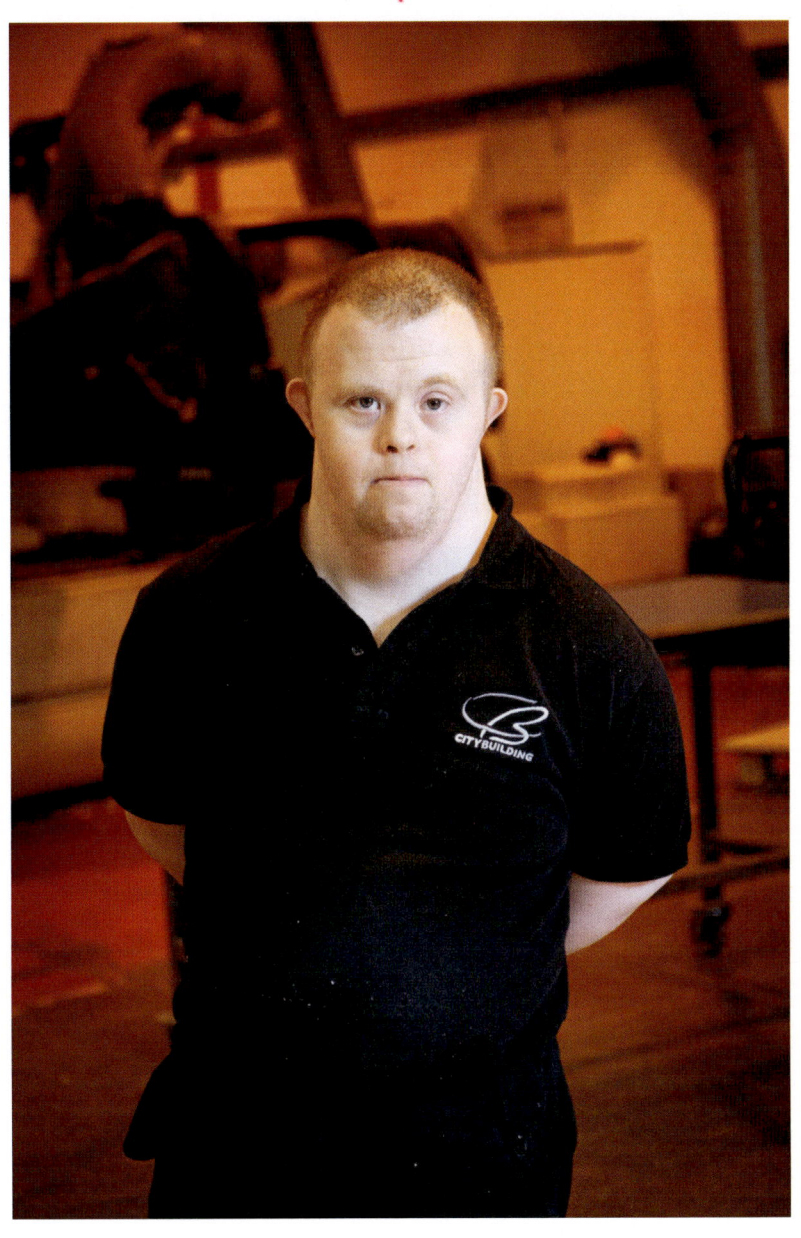

Barry Ward, Community

John Kane, National Union of Mineworkers

Chand Kausar, Pharmacists' Defence Association

Left: Neil Patterson, Musicians' Union
Right: Frederic Bayer, UNISON

Callum Youngson, Fire Brigades Union

Ewan Fergus, Fire Brigades Union

Kieran Oliveira, Fire Brigades Union

Denise Christie, Fire Brigades Union

Andy Brown, Unite the Union

Left: Lukasz Banaszek, Prospect
Right: David Cowley, Prospect

Joyce McMillan (left) and Mark Fisher (right)
National Union of Journalists

Left: Joshua Morris, STUC Youth Committee
Right: Careworker, GMB

Layla-Roxanne Hill, National Union of Journalists

Louise Gilmore, GMB

Rozanne Foyer, General Secretary STUC

Ane Miren Zelaia Arieta-Araunabena, ELA (Basque Workers Solidarity)

Pauline Rourke, STUC President 2022 and Communication Workers Union

Stewart Wakelam-Munro, Unite the Union

Georgina Brown, Prospect

Fiona McCulloch, GMB

Sandra Milligan, GMB

Euan Lynch (left) and Mark Ross (right), Educational Institute of Scotland

Tom Donnelly, Educational Institute of Scotland

Left: Scott Middleton, Communication Workers Union
Right: John McAlinden, Communication Workers Union

Left: Graeme Russell, Communication Workers Union
Right: Alison McCaig, Prospect

Darren Burns, Communication Workers Union

Fatima Jawara, Equity

Michael Mackenzie, Equity

Paul Hanlon, Scottish Professional Footballers Association

Rab Noakes, Musicians' Union

Stephen Greenhorn, Scottish Society of Playwrights

Jenny Douglas, Unite the Union

Maureen Scott, Royal College of Midwives

Amanda Alonso, CCOO Catalunya
(National Workers Commission Union of Catalonia)

Tony Adams, Educational Institute of Scotland

Adela Mansur, Educational Institute of Scotland

PART 3

Ideas Worth Fighting For

IT IS TRUE that beams of light can be found in those losses trade unionists have wallowed in. Similarly, from the most perilous of circumstances come great expressions of hope. Roses grow from the ashes. So it is that here we have the stories of virtue wrought from the ruinous miners' strike, exhilarating solidarity through scything pension cuts, and workers wresting control during Thatcherite excess.

Such deeds snare across the world. There is righteously angry unity in Bhopal and eyes opened and help given where it can be in Palestine. Fellowship with the Colombian oppressed and those made to flee Chile can be found too. Personal heartbreak leads to remembrance of workers everywhere and a refusal to rest until laws shift. Solidarity and internationalism appear every bit as important to the trade unionist as terms and conditions.

These stories also embrace unexpected territories for trade union pursuits – football, art, prisons – and the vital nitty-gritty of committee work. There are salutes to the power of learning, and of using the past positively. They recount endeavours to make this a better country for the old, and to oppose racism and fascism then, now and in the future. These facets too are about striving hard in the cause of others until a better day comes.

Here, then, are tales of eking good from bad and the enduring power of ideas worth fighting for.

Black Workers' Committee
Anita Shelton

In 1997, Anita was among a number of trade unionists asked by the STUC's Bill Speirs to form a standing Black Workers' Committee. It would campaign for the rights of BAME workers in Scotland, and on the societal issues they faced outside the workplace.

THE IDEA WAS that leading on from the establishment of the St Andrew's Day March and Rally, something needed to be done within the trade union movement to improve conditions for black workers and ensure solidarity between all workers in the Scottish trade union movement. So the STUC Black Workers' Committee (BWC) was born.

When we started, there were increased racist activities by groups such as the National Front in Scotland. That's what we were faced with. We met at the STUC offices on Woodlands Terrace, and we developed three or four organising committees. Our first conference took place in November 1997 and it has continued annually since then.

Solidarity among black people in Scotland in previous times has been somewhat difficult, in part because there were so few black people here. When I came to Scotland at the end of 1990, days could pass and I would see Asians, but no people of Caribbean or African descent. We were scattered here and there. As far as I knew, I was the first black person to work in my place of employment in a professional capacity.

In terms of the issues we faced and still face, racism was and is prevalent. It is something that I deal with every day. I was racially assaulted in 2002 by a group of men and women in the centre of Glasgow, on my way to chair a trade union committee meeting at John Smith House. That was tough but what appalled me was that no-one in the long line of traffic on West Campbell Street came to find out if I was OK as I lay there. It still takes my breath away to think of that experience.

The big issue between when we started and now remains denial. There has been a history of denial of race issues in Scotland, and these can no longer be tucked away safely. They have now been repeatedly challenged in workplaces throughout the country. In the early days it had more to do with recruitment, which is still an issue, but now the situation is more about discrimination in terms of career progression. This is really very serious in Scotland for minority ethnic people.

The Committee did face difficulties when we began. Within the trade union movement, there was a negative reaction from some. There was not universal agreement and acceptance of the concept of a BWC. There were some unions that were quite reticent in terms of supporting contractual arrangements for representation and offering financial support to reimburse delegates at conferences and the like. But after it was shown that we were here to stay, and also that we were doing good work, nearly all of them relented.

It was agreed early on that we would pay attention and advocate on issues that were not specifically labour force participation issues, but were issues of extreme importance to black people in Scotland, workers and residents alike. The first big issue of this type was the Chhokar Campaign, the result of a horrific murder. And now, unfortunately, a similar situation has developed around the Sheku Bayoh case. Sheku was killed being restrained by police in Fife in 2015. That case is still outstanding and the Committee continues to campaign.

The BWC will, of course, continue its campaigns on terms and conditions in the employment area. Covid has highlighted some important deficits in the UK, at large, and Scotland, in particular. One of these concerns the physical and mental health of the BAME population. I saw a report that indicated that there was no statistical base upon which Scotland could accurately analyse the effects and impacts of Covid on minority ethnic populations, and I mean not only black people, but all ethnic minorities, which really is appalling. Researchers can hide behind the notion that they are portraying anonymity in their work and not coming to any conclusions in a prejudicial sense. However, when it comes to health, education, and some of the real barometers of the quality of our society here, we must collect and document this information.

Another topic that might be on the horizon soon is the issue of reparations for this country's part in the slave trade. Because of Scotland's role, there could be substantial impact here. The BWC's input on that topic would be important. On the BWC there are a variety of countries and cultures represented, some of which have been impacted to this day by the slave trade. In education, the Curriculum for Excellence still doesn't incorporate or enable enough emphasis or pathways concerning Scotland's true role in the chattel slave trade.

One of the most important things about the BWC has been the sense of integration and solidarity among black workers in Scotland that it has fostered. That has been tremendous. With Black Lives Matter anti-racism campaigns and increasing public support – encouraged and demanded by the BWC and many other national and international campaigning warriors – as Angela Davis has said: this is, indeed, a moment of possibility.

Resistance, unity and pensions
Cat Boyd

In 2010, Cat – now PCS National Officer for Scotland – started working for the DWP in Glasgow. She became a union rep and joined the Coalition of Resistance, which brought together anti-austerity activists from across the city. During the 2011 public sector pensions dispute, solidarity bloomed.

WHEN THE 2010 General Election returned a coalition government and the austerity plan was outlined, through various factors I got back in touch with some of my friends from the anti-war movement who'd been involved in student politics after I'd left university, and they were starting an anti-austerity campaign, which I got involved with.

As a trade union rep, I tried to tailor some of that anti-austerity action towards what was happening to people in the public sector at that time – pay freezes, erosion of terms and conditions and of course big cuts to pensions.

In Scotland we operated the Coalition of Resistance with a little bit of autonomy. We worked from the old STUC building on Woodlands Road in Glasgow. I'll be forever grateful to the STUC for their patience, letting these young radges and radicals use that space, and us often being late with the bills.

We were driven by a concept of joining together three fronts of defence against the austerity programme. There were students, enraged by the Liberal Democrat U-turn on tuition fees.

There were people like me who were engaged in workplace struggles over pay and pensions and the chipping away of terms and conditions. And then there were people from fairly well-connected working-class communities who were at the sharp edge of privatisation and closure of services, benefit cuts and restructuring. We wanted to work out a way that we could link these three strands together, and that was part of the whole Coalition of Resistance project.

We got a lot of donations from trade unions but we would also do our own fundraising – me and an activist friend ran a sponsored 10k to try and raise money so we could pay for our placards, pay our bills at the STUC and print leaflets. A lot of the fundraising was very ad hoc, but it was a lot of fun. I also remember selling football cards in the pub across the road from my workplace, the Station Bar. This was all to raise money for the campaign, but particularly for a bus, which we rented for strike days.

We wanted these three groups to get to know each other and work together and recognise that our struggles were intertwined with each other; even though we might have specific battles we were fighting one big war. If there was a demonstration coming up, we would all make placards together on an assembly line in the STUC building. You would have this opportunity to chat to people, a chance for camaraderie, which was often joyful, even whilst things were getting tough for folk. We didn't want people making big speeches, we wanted people in working groups, and everything to be action-based rather than those history lesson style meetings you often get with left-wing groups.

We would break people into three themed groups based on questions like 'How are we going to organise this student demo next week?', 'What kind of solidarity can we show to workers who are going on strike?' and 'How can we help in the East End, we're they're trying to close the Accord day centre for adults with learning disabilities?' Then we asked people to go to a group for 40 minutes and come up with a collective action plan, and then present it back. I had heard from my parents about things like the miners' strike so I knew about the word solidarity, but not what it felt like. Now I did.

A lot of this culminated in the first strike about cuts to public sector pensions in June 2011. There was a 4.30am start and we had covered all the entrances to the DWP benefits centre in Glasgow, my workplace. We were there, we were prepared and me and my friend had made this huge banner about the pensions strike. They were raising the pension age at the time and so our banner said: 'Work Until You Die? Strike Until You Win!'

The weather was decent that day and there was this real buzz. Hardly anybody was crossing the picket line. After two or three hours, you start to get tired, and people do cross, and you talk to them and it's hard when that happens. And then at about 7.30am – and I knew what was about to happen, I'd been involved in the planning – I heard this bus engine and this absolute racket, and I saw it coming down from behind Cowcaddens and coming along the street. It was this bus that the Coalition of Resistance had hired. It was actually one of the open top, red double decker buses that do the city tour.

It was decked out in every union banner and there were people out with megaphones. All the students were on it and all the community activists from the East End. They came off the bus with tea, coffee and rolls. Every striker got a drink and a roll. There was this carnival atmosphere. The boost to morale was incredible. It was so exciting. Here was a real-life example of people engaged in other struggles who were coming to this picket line about pensions. They saw their struggles were similar, they felt that solidarity and it was beautiful.

We continued to build for the strike in November, which was obviously going to be much bigger – the biggest since the 1920s, in fact. There was a huge build up to that day, November 30th. There was an early picket line, drums, people banging pots and pans. I stood with a woman who I will always be indebted to in terms of my trade unionism – Pam Atabu, who was branch secretary at the Glasgow benefits PCS branch. Pam passed away a few years ago and I'm getting emotional thinking about it. Pam was short and she had this huge mass of this brilliant red hair. She was a force of nature. She was one of those women who almost grab you and they say: 'You go for it. You go, and you organise, and you do what you have to do.'

Pam encouraged fresh ideas. She was in her 40s then. But I have this memory of her on the picket line when a colleague of hers, who was a union member, who had been promoted through the DWP, crossed the picket line in his car. Pam was like, 'Bill, please listen, don't do this. This is us. It's you and me and all these other people.' He had his window down and he said, 'Pam, I'm so sorry, I'll be given such a hard time if I don't go in.' He carried on, the barrier went up, and his car disappeared into the car park. I saw the look on her face. She looked pale and drawn and sad. There was this lull. And then, about 60 seconds later, you heard this car approach from behind. It came up to us. It was Bill and he wound his window down. 'I can't fucking do it,' he said. Then he got out and he was on the picket line. It was a moment of solidarity and it was a beautiful thing to see.

The bus came down again and it was something else. It was even busier than before. It had been doing a tour of all the picket lines. It had been to colleges and all sorts of workplaces. It was stuffed full. There was singing, mostly unpublishable things; it was incredible. These people coming off the bus did not know the names of the people on the picket lines and vice versa, but no-one cared. It was a case of 'I know you because this is our fight.'

Being in a union shows the power of unity in action. Experiencing that changes people's lives. It makes us a force to be reckoned with.

Fighting for older workers
Elinor McKenzie and Helen Biggins

Elinor and Helen are retired teachers. They are also lifelong activists who in recent years have put their expertise and campaigning zeal into the work of the Scottish Pensioners' Forum, an independent group initiated by the STUC Pensioners' Committee.

Helen: When I was a little girl, my mother was left a widow because my father died two weeks before I was born in a mining accident, in 1930. I was the youngest of six children and she was left with all of us on her own. She immediately began an active political life by going out demonstrating on the issue of widows' pensions, and then had all of us involved with all of these demonstrations in trying to get a Labour MP into parliament. That was when I became aware of groups that stood up and gave a voice to working people.

Elinor: I don't remember a time when I didn't know about trade unions. I was born in January 1943 into family of Communist Party of Great Britain (CPGB) members. In 1956 I joined the Young Communist League and the CPGB. Both my parents were union members, and other family members too. Principles were part of everyday life. For instance, D.C. Thompson publications were not allowed in the house as that employer was known as anti-union. So, no *Sunday Post* or Thomson comics. *The Daily Worker* was the paper of choice.

Family outings and occasions seemed to coincide with political events. For example, the Burns Supper we attended had the traditional trappings but also discussions of Burns the democrat. The suffragette and communist Helen Crawford is buried in my village, Eaglesham, and every year we would place flowers on her grave on International Women's Day. Every May Day, my sister and I would travel to Glasgow for the parade, and I can remember meeting Paul Robeson there. There were other things too – the *Daily Worker* Bazaar and The Socialist Sunday School, held in the premises of the Indian Workers' Association, at Gorbals Cross. For years, we were the only communists in the village and well known. So it was an interesting childhood!

Helen: My first direct link with trade unionism was when I was a student, doing my teaching training. We were all introduced to the EIS, which was a sort of 'posh' version of a trade union. That was when I started taking an interest. I realised then that if you banded together as a large group, it stopped you being isolated whenever you had an issue that you wanted to raise, and it gave you the strength of a community of like-minded workers. It wasn't just about raising contentious issues in your workplace, but also about organising the way in which workers related to their employers, and vice versa.

Elinor: Aged 15, I left school and I started work as a junior administrative assistant in the personnel department at Weir's of Cathcart in Glasgow. I joined the Clerical and Administrative Workers Union. Part of my job was to attend union/management meetings to assist with minutes and photocopying. I noted the brutal way in which Weir's ended a long-standing bonus scheme, leading to significant losses of income for most workers. My experience at Weir's was a huge learning curve. It taught me the need for union's and collective bargaining to protect and improve workers' standard of living.

Helen: I remember as a teacher the early times I went out on strike and marching. I can recall having that feeling of the strength of the union being with you. We went out underneath our exquisite, beautiful EIS banner, which had a Latin motto, and all of the teachers behind it were trying to translate it! None of us could get a handle around it, even the Latin teachers.

As a rep I can remember taking part in talks with our employers about our pay and conditions. I always saw that part of trade unionism as the major part. It oiled the wheels of everything by allowing a spokesperson to negotiate conditions with employers. That was the major part of the work of trade unions and I feel that because we concentrate on major issues, we forget about the huge amount of great work done by trade union employees and reps in negotiating on a daily basis on behalf of workers to ensure that their salaries and conditions live up to the work that they do. That valuable role should be respected and spoken about more.

Elinor: A landmark trade union moment in my life was living with my young family in Clydebank during the UCS work-in. I must stress that I had no direct involvement whatsoever in the work-in, but its influence far exceeded the boundaries of the yards. Local shops had collection cans on their counters, and children collected lemonade bottles for refund, added their pocket money, and lined up at the yard gates to donate to the UCS fund. There was a surge in working-class consciousness. There were conversations at the shops and on buses. Confidence and hope were very real in the workplace and in the wider community. And this was sustained long enough for it to contribute to the later demand for a Scottish Assembly – an important move in the history of the democratisation of the British state.

Helen: The issue I remember becoming really passionate about was the miners' strike. I was able to co-operate with some of the supporters of the miners in ensuring that they were able to receive help and support during that long strike. And then there was the nurses' strike, when teachers all came out in support of the nurses. That one did end well, because we succeeded in getting a much-improved offer for nurses at the time. Of course, Maggie Thatcher made that kind of supporting of other unions' actions unlawful.

Elinor: The Scottish Pensioners' Forum (SPF) was established in 1992 as an umbrella organisation for all groups and individuals working and campaigning for a better deal for older people in Scotland.

The STUC played the lead role in setting up the SPF, which was enabled by monies remaining from the Dundee Timex dispute fund. From the outset, the vision was for an older peoples' organisation which was broad in its membership, embracing trade unionists, pensioner organisations, minority ethnic groups, churches, and all shades of the political spectrum in Scotland. This vision has been maintained and is reflected in the membership today. The SPF is affiliated to the National Pensioners' Convention which operates in a similar way in England and Wales. We work together on reserved matters and campaigns of common interest.

Helen: We've run quite a number of campaigns to try and give a voice to older people. I remember demonstrating about concessionary travel, when it seemed to be threatened, and we went through to the Scottish Parliament and demonstrated outside there and won that one. We demonstrated outside the BBC building in Glasgow on free television licenses for over 75s when they were under threat. We also demonstrated for pensioners when the 'huge' rise we were given was 75p. We've demonstrated because we wanted to see the removal of standing charges on electricity and gas in order to make life financially less burdensome on older people. We're still campaigning because of reports of bullying and harassment in employment for older people. We are engaged in talks with the Scottish Government on the setting up of the National Care Service, taking part in the consultations they're having.

Elinor: The SPF has been active over the years putting our views to a range of politicians. We have also taken part in many campaigns for example VAT on fuel, Post Office closures, age discrimination and funeral poverty. There have been a number of pensions campaigns too – Restore the Link, Fair Pensions, Stop Robin' the Pensioners, Pensions Justice for Women.

We have attended many events too, such as the There is a Better Way STUC march in Edinburgh, the People First STUC demonstration in Glasgow, the March for the Alternative in London, the STUC Cost of Living Crisis rally, and anti-racist events.

Poverty, health and social care, housing and transport are huge issues for older people today. Inadequate pensions and funding for services mean that younger family members – usually women – sacrifice their job prospects and overall development to provide a free service for which their parents have already paid in advance.

Older people do not want to turn back the equality clock for women. Poverty pay and underemployment leads to poverty pensions.

Nor can we allow older people to be at the mercy of private organisations that operate in the health and care sector to make a profit. Our society as a whole has spread the risk and cost of providing welfare services across the population through the use of taxation. Why should this not apply to the care of older people? The SPF does not want to retain or develop services at the expense of other groups with valid needs.

Helen: The health and wellbeing of people coming towards retirement is often ignored in a major way, and that was only too obvious in the early parts of the pandemic, when older people who were going into hospital were acquiring Covid-19 and then being thrown out to their care homes, where they infected everybody else. That was simply because government and service providers were not giving the priority status to older people's care as they should have been doing. There was a lot of talk, but in actual fact real care in valuing older people and their families, who suffered thereby, was totally ignored.

Old people are so often ignored, which makes the SPF so important. The SPF watches the way life is going for retired people, and they see the various obstacles that older people meet when they're trying to live well in terms of their financial, housing and travel needs and everything else like that.

Elinor: As we talk, we are in the middle of a cost of living crisis, with food and energy prices rising and rising and making pensioner poverty even worse. Many older people will die in this crisis unless politicians at Holyrood and Westminster act now. The number of cold-related premature deaths – or as we say, poverty-related deaths – can fluctuate between years. Across the winter 2017 to 2018 the figure was just under 60,000 and in 2018 to 2019 it was around 30,000 in the UK. The note attached to those statistics reads: 'We may assume that hypothermia is the primary cause of cold-related death, whilst the greatest impact is among older age groups.'

This cost of living crisis is not one that will be felt equally. Those in poverty already spend the highest share of their incomes on daily essentials. There is little slack left. Well-meaning 'tips to get by' – such as wearing another jumper, a woolly hat, socks, turning your heating boiler down, storing hot water in a flask – just won't cut it!

We need living wages and pensions. We need a government willing to take on the energy giants, the food industry, the private health and care providers, the arms trade. The cost of living crisis is a class issue and must not be defined as a personal problem. Our priority must be to fight for a future that is based on solidarity and dignity. In the 21st century we can no longer live in a society defined by extreme inequality. We must collectively act to prevent the further impoverishment of the working class. That is the position of the Scottish Pensioners Forum.

An issue now getting all trade unionists across the generations to see how pensions must be kept high up the agenda of our campaigning. Pensioners on their own are not going to be able to establish the dignity and respect and security that they deserve in old age having produced much of the wealth throughout their working lives. We know that it is the trade union movement that we have to turn to in order to better the experience of our older people. No other group will do it.

We want to be part of the fight for better future conditions for everybody, including those coming up behind us. It's important we don't lose all of the gains that have been made over the years. Nothing has been given to us, we've had to fight and struggle for it. The trade unions have been to the fore of all these struggles. That's a big reason why the SPF maintain their link.

Women's Committee prison visit

Janet Cassidy

Janet worked on the railways, initially as a guard. In 1992, she became one of Scotland's first female train drivers. She was also on the STUC's Women's Committee. Here, she recalls a fact-finding prison visit which was part of a Committee probe into violence against women.

IN FEBRUARY 2005, when the visit took place, I was Chair of the STUC Women's Committee. Mary Senior, then the Committee's Assistant Secretary, and I went up to Cornton Vale, in Stirling. The idea was to find out what went on in Scotland's only women's prison. It's not something you associate day to day with the trade union movement. It was a learning curve for Mary and I.

First we had a meeting with the Prison Governor, some officials from the Scottish Prison Officers' Association and some staff members. We heard about some of the problems inmates here had – there were high drug and alcohol addiction numbers and mental health issues. Then we went on a tour of the prison.

It was enlightening, the first time I'd ever been involved with a prison. The prison seemed very outdated. I was surprised at the amount of women in there because they hadn't paid their television licence. And the amount of very young women inside shocked me. They were often there through drugs. It opens your eyes because you're sitting in your own wee world, getting on with life, and you don't give these things a thought.

The officers treated us really well. We had a guided tour through the prison, but we didn't get to talk to any of the prisoners. We saw inside some cells, and the family centre, the chaplain area and the hairdressing salon and laundry, where some of the women worked.

When we got to the final part of the tour, we could see the people who helped rehabilitate and retrain prisoners – housing advisors and other things – so at least when they were released there was a chance they wouldn't go back in.

There is always a stigma for prisoners when they are released. They find it hard to come by work because of their records. If you haven't worked for so many years, a new employer is going to ask what the gap in your employment is from. Maybe trade unions could help with that. I know there are some crimes that you cannot forgive, but at the time some of the things the women were locked up for seemed almost petty. It's sad – whatever happened to a second chance?

By artists, for artists
Janie Nicoll and Lynda Graham

How people work has changed immeasurably this century. Many more are self-employed and toil in often precarious freelance fields. Artists are a case in point. Here, Janie and Lynda from the Scottish Artists' Union, one of the STUC's newest members, talk about their sector.

Lynda: I've grown up with a sense of trade unions because my grandfather was a shop steward in the engineering industry. I joined the Scottish Artists' Union (SAU) because I was appalled at the treatment of freelance artists and thought instead of moaning that I should do something about it. I got involved on the Executive Committee as the union is artist-led – at that time it only had one part-time member of staff, so all of the work apart from processing memberships was done by the voluntary committee and it was a good opportunity to become active. It was also inspiring to see the achievements of previous committee members.

Janie: When I was a student at Edinburgh College of Art in the '80s, we had a 'work-in' – an occupation of the college over the threats to student grants. We took over the college and locked out the Principal and staff that weren't supportive. It was an amazing thing to be part of – for the students to take control of the buildings, we even slept there. The occupation lasted three days and we got a lot of news coverage. At that point I realised you could speak up at meetings and be vocal. I understood the power of collective action.

The SAU was begun in 2001 by a handful of artists. I thought I should get involved as I believed in the basic principles of getting organised and trying to improve things for artists. My membership number is 21, so I was in the first group. I felt that no matter what happened with it, it was important.

As a freelancer you're on your own – no salary, no normal worker's rights like sick pay – so being part of a union for artists is really important. We're pretty much dealing with the gig economy and the only way that we can make improvements is to join together and take collective action. As freelancers you are competing for every contract or project, but you have to stand back and take a broader overview, and that's what the union is dealing with. People are joining because they want to be part of something; part of a union of artists. They like that idea.

Lynda: When we first started up, we were very much a servicing union and not a campaigning one, or the campaigns were more sporadic. We had a review by an independent organisation – Hack Aye – in 2016, and the membership voted in favour of its recommendations. That meant moving from being a service union to become more campaigning and activist-based.

We weren't members of the STUC before that review, and shortly afterwards we were accepted for membership. That brought with it access to support, and in 2018 we got funding for a learning programme through the STUC's Scottish Union Learning, which expanded quickly across Scotland. It means we're able to offer workshops and events for artists and makers across a range of subject matter, supporting them not just to survive within the existing system – like how to do your books or run a workshop – but also looking more broadly at the arts eco-system, and at inequalities and how we can address them. More recently we've talked about things like climate change, sustainability, and inter-sectional approaches – issue-based topics where we ask how we can influence broader change.

People still join for the practical things we offer, but now we're developing a collective sense of solidarity so we can pressurise politicians and others to improve conditions for artists, rather than just surviving within the sector as it is. We are trying to affect change. Pay rates have been a big driver and in 2021, we introduced template contracts for artists to use.

Janie: The Fair Work project we were part of helped us to create those bespoke contacts with the help of solicitors. We felt that along with the issue of pay rates – and it took Creative Scotland 10 years to take on our recommended rates of pay – the main issue was that so many artists don't have decent contracts and are at the mercy of other people's contracts. We worked to create bespoke contracts that artists can use and they give the artist more control over projects and over working conditions, for example when they're exhibiting work.

We had a campaign called Seeing Red, which was based on the results of a member survey. That was about how the arts had been treated during the pandemic. Members felt angry about the number of people who had fallen through the net and not qualified for government support. They were left high and dry. We got artists to send us their red images and we did a social media splurge. That kind of campaigning, and using visual platforms like Instagram, has raised our profile and gained us more members.

Lynda: The pandemic actually opened up some doors in terms of working with other unions. We now have regular meetings between the Creative Industries Affiliate unions – Musicians' Union, Equity, Bectu and others – and they are really useful. We have pre-meetings where we are able to strategise, talk about our common issues and raise them with the Scottish Government, Creative Industries staff and sector representatives. During the Covid-19 pandemic, it was a good way to be able to pin down exactly what was happening with support for our members and tell the government what was working for our members and what wasn't.

Janie: Ultimately, we are an artists' union set up by artists and run for them. We know the issues and that's part of our strength.

Helping the firefighters of Palestine

Jim Malone

Jim is a retired fireman from Dundee. The end of active service, though, has not stopped his heartfelt internationalist commitment to helping firefighters in Palestine.

IN 1982, ISRAEL launched the invasion of Lebanon, which led to various massacres and the expulsion of the Palestine Liberation Organisation (PLO) from that country to north Africa. The Fire Brigades Union (FBU) general secretary at the time was the great Ken Cameron. He became the first trade unionist at TUC Congress to raise a motion that actually criticised Israel. He did it forcibly and with support from the Trade Union Friends of Palestine (TUFP).

The TUFP had been formed in Dundee in 1979. A year later, the city twinned with the municipality of Nablus on the occupied West Bank. So we Dundonians had that link and I was fully aware of it before I joined the fire service. Back then, I was a painter and decorator and a UCATT member. Then I joined the brigade and the FBU and became a union official and realised the importance of the international campaigns. There was also the strong support of the Dundee TUC for those campaigns and the twinning, so we were always being kept up to date by them about the on-going occupation of Palestine by Israel.

One of the members of the STUC delegation to Palestine in 2008 was our secretary in Scotland, Kenny Ross. He came back with the idea of bringing some firefighters from Nablus to Dundee – he had visited the Nablus fire station. In 2009, we brought over the Nablus Eight and that included some training at Gullane and Perth. They received their diplomas for training here.

That gave us the impetus to do something more. We wanted to see if we could purchase fire appliances for them. I had been elected Scottish Organiser of the FBU and our international plan was to take our idea to conference to see if we could get funds. We did that and we bought two fire appliances from Tayside Fire and Rescue. In 2011, we filled them with kit and we decided to drive the 2,500 miles to Piraeus port in Athens. Then we would deliver them to Palestine.

One of the fire engines was involved in an accident in Greece. We had anticipated problems because although they were well-maintained, they were old appliances. So we left one there, and two of the lads drove the remaining one onto the boat, while some of us flew to Israel. There, we were involved in negotiations including with the British Embassy to see if we could secure the safe passage of the appliance to Palestine. Israeli customs impounded the vehicle and all the kit, and took all the supplies we'd brought for the refugee camps.

In December, through the support of the Israeli Histadrut group who had put pressure on the Israeli authorities, and with the UK and Scottish parliaments also pressurising through diplomatic channels, we managed to get that appliance full of kit delivered to Nablus.

Following that visit, we decided to embark upon a further training programme. We went through a Cross Party Group in the Scottish Parliament. Since then we've trained in Scotland the officer corps of the Palestinian Civil Defence, and separately the municipality fire services like Nablus, Hebron, Jerusalem and Ramallah.

As trade unionists, we always seek to represent our members by giving them the conditions that allow them to work with dignity, and also to provide the humanitarian assistance to the community we serve. As a firefighter, that's at the forefront and it is one of your sacred vows when you join – 'to render humanitarian assistance', we say that in the oath. But trade unionism makes you identify the need to fight injustice whether it appears here or internationally. The movement in this country has always had a strong voice across the world as a power for good.

To me, Palestine was a stain on the United Kingdom. The history of the occupation of the Holy Land and how it was put together and the line in the sand; if you read the books, you'll realise that this is an oozing, seeping sore and a horrible legacy. So we must fight for justice for Palestinians. Their children are no different from our children.

The firefighters we have tried to support through the FBU and the STUC are the same as firefighters everywhere. We all perform a humanitarian task, in every corner of the globe. Unfortunately, due to the military occupation of their lands, these Palestinians can't do that very easily.

In 2019, there were three kids in a house in Hebron, all from the one family. They were all killed in a fire while the Israelis kept the Palestinian firefighters at a checkpoint. They were in view of this fire. Can you imagine being a firefighter looking at a house on fire and being kept away by the police? There would be a riot here. But this is what the Palestinian firefighters are subjected to. They are humanitarians trying to save lives, being denied that opportunity. We tell politicians this and they can hardly believe it, while at the same time they are providing tax breaks for companies building missiles here in Scotland.

So we're not gonna be stepping back.

Visiting Palestine

Liz Elkind

A New Yorker who moved to Edinburgh in 1975, Liz became active in the trade union movement here. As a member of Edinburgh Trades Union Council and the STUC General Council, she was invited to visit Palestine as part of a fact-finding STUC delegation in 2009.

I AM JEWISH AND I am very privileged to have had a very sceptical mother. My mother never really bought into 'a land without people for a people without land.' When my sister and I were kids, we wanted to be like all the other kids, but when they came around asking us for a dollar to contribute to the building fund or a tree in Israel, my mother wasn't happy. She was a sceptic but she was also very frightened in terms of taking a line that was very different to the prevailing line for Jews in America. She didn't like falling out with people, she couldn't do it, so she kept quiet but she was not willing for her kids to be carried away on this idea.

When I came to Scotland I became aware that there were other people who were sceptical or who wanted to know more. I was a member of the Communist Party, which I was involved in in New York too, and I also became friendly with a group of people in Edinburgh called Palestine Action. I started learning and reading and I wanted to go to Palestine.

A visit to Palestine had long been argued for by me and other members of the STUC General Council. Solidarity with Palestine had been on the STUC's agenda at congresses for many years. In 2008, a motion was passed saying that there should be a delegation. The Palestine visit was about internationalism and solidarity, which was right up my street and how I was brought up. I first went to Palestine with a friend who had contacts from an earlier trip, and we went for a fortnight in 2008. I was desperate to return. I was in ecstasy when the STUC invited me on their 2009 visit.

The aim was to make contact with trade unionists on both sides of the divide. Some of us really wanted to engage those who were in trade union leadership positions back here on the Palestine issue. We hoped the people who went would learn something, and that learning might help engage them in bringing the STUC closer in their solidarity position with Palestine. Having previously visited, I could recommend some things we should see and do. For instance, with the STUC delegation we went on an Alternative Political Tour I had already been on.

Jerusalem is made up of lots of surrounding villages. In one we visited the Israelis had put an enormous pipe right through the middle in a ditch with fences surrounding it – this was before the wall had been finished. I had seen the previous year children coming home from school having to come through the pipe because otherwise it was a one and a half hour walk around it. This time, I saw that the Israelis had put up screens so that the kids couldn't do that. Even thinking about it now upsets me.

We visited the Israeli trade unionists who had organised our visit. They were very corporate. But it was nice to meet them, and they were very welcoming. We were taken to meet some civil servants right after Operation Cast Lead – a three-week war in the Gaza Strip. We had a lunch and then they stood up to welcome us and talk. They showed us this plan in various colours. Essentially what they were saying was, 'We've been criticised for bombing buildings that people were living in Gaza City, but if you can see here, you can see we just aimed at the corners of the buildings.' My recollection is that they knew at that moment they had lost us. Very shortly after that there was a decision made that we would end the Israeli part of the trip early and move to the Palestinian part of the trip.

Then we went to Nablus. We weren't allowed to take the minibus we'd been using there as the driver wasn't allowed outside Jerusalem. We had to take another bus from outside the Greater Jerusalem border. We went through a couple of checkpoints. Nablus was a wonderful place to visit in terms of sights and sounds. I loved the street cries and the sounds of the mosques. The people we met there from the Palestinian General Federation of Trade Unions (PGFTU) were professional but not corporate. They were interested in what we were learning and what we had seen. The general secretary of the PGFTU took us on a very personal tour of Nablus, including to his birthplace.

We had to divide up because there were two different visits one day. I went with two other people who worked in education – as I did – to a university. That was an interesting visit to a beautiful campus. However, there were many things that made me so sad and angry.

Some students would be late for class because they had gone through humiliations when they were stopped at the border and they'd had their books taken away, and young men had been asked to strip. Then when they came to class they had to explain what had happened. One woman, a teacher, said to us, 'I'm glad you are here, but so what, what are you going to do when you get back? People keep coming here. We have delegation after delegation in Palestine, then what happens?' That was devastating. And it was true.

I was honoured to move a motion based on the delegation's report to the 2009 STUC Annual Congress, which was passed unanimously.

Michael's Story and International Workers' Memorial Day

Louise Adamson

After the tragic death of her brother, Michael, in a workplace incident, former employment lawyer Louise has worked tirelessly with campaigners, trade unionists and the STUC to raise health and safety awareness and push for change in corporate killing law.

ONE ORDINARY MORNING in 2005, my brother left home for work and he didn't get home to his fiancée. He didn't get home because his health and safety wasn't looked after by his employer. Numerous failures on the site where he was working meant that a 26-year-old man with his whole life ahead of him had that life ended.

Michael didn't work in a unionised workplace. He wasn't a trade union member, his colleagues weren't trade union members. I think a difference would've been made had he been working in a trade unionised workplace. He may very well still be here today.

He wasn't provided with the right equipment to do his job safely. Risk assessments weren't kept up to date, management and supervision was abysmal on the site where he was working, and that all led to a sort of perfect storm where he cut a cable that was labelled 'not in use' and in fact it was wired into a distribution board and he suffered a fatal electric shock.

His employer was subsequently charged with health and safety offences, as were a managing director, an operations director and a technical services manager. The three individuals ended up walking free from the dock because the prosecutor made errors. So it was the employer, the company, who were called 'The Invisible Man' by their lawyers, that were found guilty of the failures that led to Michael's death. And it was The Invisible Man that was fined £300,000 as a result, which is not justice. It doesn't provide my family with anything in the way of comfort.

That's why I'm trying to use Michael's story to try and effect change, and to get employers to wake up to their health and safety responsibilities, before something like this happens.

After a tragedy like that occurs, you have to decide what's best. Some people go for counselling and that helps them. It didn't help me. I needed to know that a difference was going to be made as a result of what happened to Michael; that positive things were going to come from something that was so awful. Initially it was about getting us the legal help we needed to support us through the prosecution process.

But then one day working in the employment law job I did, I came across a TUC email announcing the launch of this new group called Families Against Corporate Killers (FACK), and it was a group that had been set up by individuals that had been bereaved by work, and they were looking to support other families, and to make a difference through what had happened to their loved ones.

I popped an email to them and that was a real turning point. They were able to point me in the direction of help in Scotland. I was initially given contact details for Ian Tasker, who was at the STUC, and Ian was amazing from the start.

At that time, about 16 years ago, there were moves to change the law on corporate homicide. Ian was able to get me involved in all sorts of things – attending meetings, then speaking at some events about what happened to Michael and to other families. Through getting to know Ian, the STUC and Scottish Hazards, I began to give talks and deliver training in workplaces about health and safety and the experiences of bereaved families like mine, and that eventually snowballed into a lot of what I deliver now as 'Michael's Story'.

It has been amazing to know that there is this day – International Workers' Memorial Day (IWMD) – that is for us. The slogan is, 'Remember the dead, fight for the living' – it's not just a remembrance memorial service, it's about renewing a commitment to effect positive change from things that have gone on in the past that shouldn't have gone on, and making sure there's no repeat in the future. Being able to speak at IWMD events and give a voice to other families who maybe don't yet feel strong enough to do that themselves has been a huge thing for me.

The 'fight for the living' element of IWMD is so important. The support that there is from the union movement around that is beyond compare. It's hugely appreciated. The work that trade union safety reps do within workplaces is incredible – every time I speak to them, I feel I can't thank them enough for what they do.

There are things that still haven't been done. The laws against corporate homicide that came in are not effective, just as we said they wouldn't be. That's still something we're pursuing through Scottish Hazards, and the STUC are giving their support to that. There needs to be change in Scotland. The law at the minute it is not a deterrent. Nor is it effective in delivering justice to families.

We have been effective in many ways, especially with how Scottish Hazards – which works with the STUC – has developed. It was a voluntary organisation but has now evolved into a workplace health and safety charity. It is the point of contact for individuals with health and safety concerns at workplaces which aren't trade unionised.

We fought for three years to get some sort of justice for Michael. Our system is certainly not set up to provide justice for people who've been bereaved at work. There's still a lot that we need to do. And I'm committed to keep working on doing it.

Another side to the miners' strike

Margot Russell

Though the miners' strike of 1984 ended in defeat, there were victories of solidarity and organisation, and moments of life-changing inspiration. Margot helped run a soup kitchen and like her friends volunteering there was politicised. She is still a local councillor today.

WHEN THE MINERS' strike began in 1984, I was winching, as we used to say, Bill, who became my husband, and he was a miner. I had no connection with the mines even though I lived in a mining area – Midlothian – but I did have colleagues whose husbands were miners, so I had a feeling for the hard work both men and women had to do to keep mining families fed. I was working as a cleaner at the Ferranti factory in Dalkeith and was a union shop steward too.

Bill advised me that the strike was happening and at that time the men were doing all the picketing. He told me that the union were trying to involve more women in the strike and suggested I go down and see what was happening with the women on the strike group, so I did. I knew some of the ladies there, and before I knew it I'd ended up being Chair! I'm not really sure how that happened and the meetings could be quite heated.

That was where we set up a soup kitchen and we had to go to the council and apply for a grant to help us buy utensils and things. As Chair I had to go and make a speech to them. They voted to give us what we needed and so the soup kitchen got started. I would work my shift at Ferranti's and then go there and help. There you were getting a different side of the story to what the news was telling you. The main channels were only really showing one side. You weren't getting a true story, apart from Channel 4 – they were fairer. But we were living it, so we knew the proper story, the human story.

It was a difficult time and the women got more and more involved. We started to go on rallies and the union gave us autonomy to have our committees, ideas, fundraising; that type of thing.

In Midlothian and all over the country, these soup kitchens were set up. We were fortunate to have a place to use in Dalkeith Miners' Club and Danderhall and Mayfield were the same. It was a good point of contact – we could speak to the families, check what was happening, ask if they needed anything.

I'd never been involved in something so huge. As time went on I realised how historic it was. It was quite an experience, especially going on rallies and going out to speak to various organisations for fundraising. It was a huge learning curve for somebody so quiet who became chair by accident. I was very quiet then. I'm not now. Seeing that I was able to do things and get a lot of support from people gave me a lot of confidence.

When the miners went back to work they were devastated. Bill's union officials had been dismissed, but they turned up at the pit to clap him and his colleagues in. I'm choking up thinking about that. I went to the soup kitchen that day not knowing what to expect. We had a chat and a cuddle.

I look back with pride that we were involved with something so historic, even if the strike was lost. There is sadness too. People lost the lives they had, families broke up. We still know who the scabs are now in our area, all those years on. There's still bitterness.

Positives? At the time I didn't think there were any. But there was a camaraderie that had been built. Leading from that there was quite a number of us who joined the Labour Party because we felt if we couldn't beat Thatcher in one way we might manage to beat her in another, via the ballot box. There was about ten of us from the soup kitchen who did that. We were comrades now. It politicised a lot of us to the injustices that existed and what could be done, if anything, to change that. A lot of them are still active, still campaigning. That's a good legacy. And eventually I became a councillor, which might be seen as a positive, though not by everybody!

Playing the union card

Michael Devlin

Stereotypes of footballers do not include their trade unionism. Yet the Professional Footballers' Association Scotland (PFAS) boasts high membership within the game. Here, vice-chairman and Scotland cap centre-back Michael explains its many vital roles.

AS A UNION we rely on senior members and reps in the changing room to recruit new players. It's about explaining why you might need the union, and why it's a good thing to be part of. As a young player, I went home once I'd heard about joining in that way and discussed it with my parents. They are both trade union people – my mum's a teacher, my dad's an engineer – and they understood the importance of it and encouraged me to join up.

Other lads, when they first come into a professional football environment, they perhaps don't see the importance of it and don't fully understand it, or think that it's not a big deal and they'll maybe join later on. I think because of that there's a responsibility on the older pros to really emphasise the key aspects of what being in a union brings, and the security it can bring. Covid is a good example of why unions are important – players heavily relied on them and their staff and lawyers and how actively they participated in negotiations with clubs on wage deferrals and cuts and threatened termination of contracts and things like that.

My passion for being a rep developed when I began to see the role a union plays. I also strongly felt that at times footballers are treated as a commodity or just a number – clubs often feel they have all the power, and to a large degree they do. Without the union you'd be in a far worse position, and that's why it's so important to join. Some of the stories players have got in touch with the SPFA about are frightening – there was a lad that played with a lower league team until recently. He tore his cruciate ligament right at the end of the season, when his contract was expiring. He was just released, no operation, no rehabilitation. He came to the union and asked what he was supposed to do – he was badly injured so he couldn't get a new club.

There is a real abdication of responsibility by clubs in situations like that in their not looking after the wellbeing of players. I feel particularly strongly about young players, and that there is no real support network if they are released by a club or leave the game completely. If you look at the statistics, very few players who are 19 or 20 are really going to progress into the first team and make it and kick on. Boys fall through the cracks all the time and there isn't much of a support network from clubs. The union plays a huge role at the point – they provide education, courses, trades and general wellbeing support.

Another area we try to tell players about is the mental health support the union can offer. There is help for gambling addiction, and other doctors and professionals who you can get in touch with. There is legal assistance, help with contractual issues and injuries – support and rehabilitation facilities for injured players.

We also cover the transition of players from full-time football to part-time football, and players coming towards the end of their careers and how they're going to transition into normal life. In Scotland, unless you're playing for Celtic and Rangers, the vast majority of players are not going to retire as comfortable gents that don't need to work. They're going to need to do something else. The union helps with that.

There are a huge amount of players who are out of the game now, unable to get back in. As a union, we need to support them as best we can. Part of that might be helping them find a club. That's a really positive thing we can do, and many players have found a route back into the game through that platform.

Would we take action like members of other unions? In terms of current issues, the union is playing an active part in trying to eradicate discrimination in football. We've seen cases of people walking off the pitch, which is a form of strike action because they're refusing to play the game. I wonder what direction that might go in as we see more cases of racist slurs from the stands, and fans booing players taking the knee. I've been part of a few phone calls, not just with the union but with other people in Scottish football, where we talk about how we're going to affect change.

As players we can only do so much, but if do we reach the point of saying 'We're not doing it, we're not playing', then we all need to stand together. We all need to do it – it's not just the case of ethnic minorities standing up; we as privileged white players need to stand up beside them, shoulder to shoulder, and as a union, to say no to racism, and that we care about this, and we must see change. That goes for sectarian abuse too, which is a huge problem in Scottish football, and homophobic terminology and language. There are a whole load of things that need to be addressed.

Players do talk about political issues. We've got a diverse bunch in the Aberdeen changing room. There was a big debate on the American election between Trump and Biden. We talk about elections, the independence referendum, whatever's going on. Societal issues need to be discussed within football. Yeah it's often a laugh and a joke and we enjoy ourselves, but serious issues are talked about. The thing I enjoy most is that players come from all sorts of backgrounds and viewpoints. A real collection, so that results in diverse opinions. I'm always in the thick of it, I try to keep it healthy so it doesn't turn into arguing. There are some deeper conversations, and there are some boys who switch off and walk out whenever those things come up. It's like any workplace from that point of view.

Learning on the job
Michelle Boyle

Aged 19, Michelle joined ScotRail as a ticket examiner. Sixteen years later, she is a guard, a Union Learning Rep and a Women's Steward in her RMT branch, and attends STUC women's and learning conferences. In 2020, she took part in a history course about women on the railway. Michelle's story demonstrates the crucial role of learning to trade unionists.

WE'D RUN A few different learning courses over Zoom during the pandemic – digital video editing, British Sign Language (BSL), Cyber Security, things like that, which the STUC had provided – and a few of us thought it'd be good to delve into the history of women in the railway and learn about that. We managed to get funding to do that. The history of the railway has always interested me. You look back and think about Glasgow Central Station, which I absolutely love.

We had 10 participants and we each brought a different topic. It was amazing because all 10 of us came up with different things, but at the same time it all went well together. For instance, one colleague came back with information about the women who worked on the railway during the wars. They worked in all sorts of roles. It had relevance to now because it is still such a male-dominated environment to work in.

In World War One, because of the times they lived in, they were expected to work on the trains wearing dresses and petticoats, which wasn't exactly safe. Four of them died when they were crushed under the wheels of trains because they were jumping onto moving trains and their dresses got caught. I was able to see that the fact we as women work on the railway now was very much down to the women then – we probably now have more female ticket examiners than male, and that came from the women who fought from that point and during the '40s, '50s and '60s to get these positions.

I've always had this fondness for learning and going into that and reading up was a great thing. It was often spinetingling. I pass the plaque in Central Station now to those who went to war from there, including the many that never came back, and it means even more now. During World War Two, 90,000 panes of glass were painted black so the Luftwaffe couldn't see it. I'm 36 and remember coming to the station as a child and wondering why it was so dark and grubby, and it was purely because those panes hadn't been replaced back then. So learning connects your personal past to the wider past. We also learned about the importance of trade unions to women in history.

Some people join a trade union in case they need support at some point or find themselves in a difficult position. But there is so much more that union dues pay for, and the fact is there are all of these courses available. Members have access to the STUC's Scottish Union Learning, access to their Union Learning Rep and if they feel they want to learn a new skill or about something, that's where we come in.

If there is demand, we can ask for support and funding. They can be interesting like the historical courses, and useful too – some of us have used what we learned on the BSL course to communicate with passengers. We also have courses for things like people who have dyslexia. Courses help you in the job and outside of it, and union membership grants you access to that. There's so much more to membership than pay negotiations and those things, important as they are. Union learning has been life-changing for me.

Anti-fascism, then and now

Mike Arnott

As Secretary of Dundee Trades Union Council, Mike has been instrumental in commemorating the role Scots played in fighting and nursing in the Spanish Civil War. Here, he explains the part of unions in recognising them and continuing to oppose fascism today.

IT'S APPROPRIATE THAt trade unions and the STUC continue to support memorials to the anti-fascist fight in Spain because they did so much fundraising and campaigning during the time of the Spanish Civil War itself. And of course, most of those who went to Spain to fight and nurse identified as trade unionists themselves.

There wouldn't be a memorial in Dundee – and an annual memorial event – if it wasn't for Dundee Trades Union Council. It's the same in Fife, Aberdeen and elsewhere; where there is a Spanish Civil War memorial or event, unions are usually present and influential. For example, every year there is an event at the La Pasionaria statue in Glasgow which is a coalition of Hope Note Hate, the People's Assembly and Unison. And in Glasgow in 2019, they unveiled a new memorial to the blockade runner crews who defied the fascist blockade of Spanish republican ports, and it was the RMT that pulled that fundraising campaign together. The commemorations are very much trade union based.

The Dundee memorial to the 16 Brigaders who had gone from the city and died in Spain was unveiled in 1985. There were a couple of spelling mistakes on it and as it turned out some men were missing so we added an extra plaque. We were able to find that out through research supported by the Dundee Trades Union Council. We produced a booklet on everyone who had gone to Spain from the city through that work too. That kickstarted us into holding an annual commemoration in Dundee. Trade unions in the region also funded a memorial over in Spain, in Tarancón, where a number of Scots died in hospital after fighting in the Battle of Jarama. So the memorials and the booklets and all of this is based on the support of trade unions and trades councils.

There has been an upsurge in interest in what the Brigaders stood for across the country. New memorials and plaques were recently built in Blantyre, Perth, Motherwell and elsewhere, often supported with trade union resources. There have been art exhibitions and plays too. It is growing – there are more people involved than ever before. The recent Fife event was the biggest it has ever been, and the general secretaries of the STUC and the GMB spoke at that. When there are appeals for something like a publication or a new memorial, or an appeal on behalf of the International Brigade Memorial Trust, the trade unions are there affiliating and donating and offering speaking spots at branch meetings. That is stronger now than it was 10 or 15 years ago.

The Motherwell memorial is enormous; they raised thousands with heavy involvement from North Lanarkshire trade unions and it's in a great spot in Duchess of Hamilton Park. But there was some fascist vandalism when someone graffitied it. Then a young lad of six or so cycled with his father from Wishaw and washed it all off. Somebody also attacked it with a hammer. So that shows we have to remain vigilant to fascism and these memorials are a symbol of that as well as of remembering what anti-fascists did in Spain.

The anti-fascist message when we have our memorial events is always in there along with the remembrance of the Brigaders and their sacrifices. It is part and parcel, as is trade union support.

A workers' newspaper

Ron McKay

In the mid-1970s, Ron was a casual journalist with the Daily Express when the closure of its Scottish operation was announced. With National Union of Journalists (NUJ) and STUC support, redundant staff formed a new worker-run broadsheet sympathetic to union causes. Robert Maxwell had other ideas...

IN 1975, BEAVERBROOKS had announced that they were closing the *Daily Express*'s Scottish operation and moving to Manchester. There were 1,900 jobs involved. They promised a waiting period but in fact almost immediately closed it. I was working as a freelance doing casual shifts. This feeling grew that a workers' co-operative should take on and re-launch a new newspaper. It coincided with the new Labour government under Harold Wilson, with Tony Benn as Industry Minister. Within six months of them getting in, they supported three workers' co-operatives, including the fledgling *Scottish Daily News* (SDN).

The deal was that that the government would go pound for pound with what the workers raised. I think they were prepared to go to £1.2m. The workers' co-operative members – about 500 of them – said they were raising the money. They had a deadline to meet, and if it wasn't it would all fall apart. Enter Robert Maxwell.

He had been a Labour MP in the '60s – not a very good one or a socialist one it has to be said – and he had failed in 1969/70 to take over the *News of the World*. He was a big player and had a thirst to be a newspaper proprietor. He came in with first of all £100,000 and as the deadline ticked down, it went up to £125,000 from him, which was necessary to meet the pound-for-pound deal with the government. So it was sold at that point.

It launched in the May of 1975, just after a May Day march.

The paper started as a broadsheet and sold maybe 300,000 copies on the first day. It was different at the beginning as it did reflect a measure of workers' control, until Maxwell's meddling doomed that. There were discussions about ways to treat stories and there was a much, much closer relationship between journalists and the ink-eaters as we called them – production workers. Prior to that the divisions were huge. I'd been on picket lines against printworkers! There was animosity between journalists and print workers, and it was so strict in those days. If you went into the Case Room or anything, you had to ask permission and you certainly couldn't touch anything, otherwise you'd be blacked and there would be an industrial dispute.

Newspaper sales declined, Maxwell stirred the pot and people by then were worried about their jobs but thought that if it all failed Maxwell would take it over and their jobs would be secure. So it relaunched as a tabloid almost overnight, but by then the rot had set in. It was under-capitalised. It wasn't able to hang on for the long haul.

The Action Committee members went to see Maxwell in his mansion, Headington Hill Hall. As well as his home it was the centre of his printing business. Ironically it was owned by Oxford City Council – so Maxwell was a council tenant, in probably the most lavish council property in the country. The Action Committee went to see him to try and get him to put money in. He invited them to sit down for tea and coffee. A flunky appeared and served them as normal, normal except for one thing: Maxwell's cup was twice as big as everybody's else's. That was symptomatic of the guy. Bombastic, overbearing, self-regarding and a crook, in the end.

Because Maxwell's money was crucial to the launch of the newspaper right from the start, and because he obviously at least put out that he would like to control the paper, there was huge amount of friction between the Workers' Council and Maxwell. It got to a ridiculous extent when he'd come on the Tannoy in the evening and berate these 'Trotskyists' and 'monsters' who were trying to destroy the whole thing. He claimed to be living and sleeping in the building, and he did have a mattress on the floor, but he was living in Central Hotel. He was all-pervasive. You would go to the canteen, and there he would be, pretending to serve.

As relations got worse, and more and more of the workforce were on Maxwell's side, there was a final mass meeting where only 12 of us voted against Maxwell – we became the Dirty Dozen. The expectation was that he was going to take it over. In fact, he just walked away. People were stunned. What had his motivation been?

The plan had been for this worker-run newspaper, but it didn't turn out that way because of Maxwell's involvement. He always had the last card and so these meetings where he was involved were always horrendous. He would come on the Tannoy later and give his side of the story. It obviously worked, and it worked because people were worried about their jobs and it worked because he was a multimillionaire and they thought the future was with him. But it went down.

In the end, 1,800 jobs went. Journalists got some redundancy payments from the NUJ and print workers got statutory redundancy. There was a vain attempt at a sit-in, at continuing the paper and selling it on the streets, but it didn't work.

Marching against racism

Satnam Ner

Prospect rep Satnam is a long-term member of the STUC Black Workers' Committee. The St Andrew's Day March they organise has become a key date in the trade union calendar, and an energetic presence in the fight against racism and fascism.

THE FIRST ST Andrew's Day march took place in 1988. I'd been working in Scotland for a couple of years. The march is particularly significant in that it signalled the start of a conscious anti-racist political effort by trade unions, led by the STUC, and involved the mobilisation of the local black community in Glasgow. The first march's sole effort was to confront the attempts by the BNP to take over St Andrew's Day in order to peddle their hatred. As a counter demonstration, it has been hugely successful.

I got more involved after attending my first STUC Black Workers' conference in 1997. It began with the march as the first session of conference. That was fabulous. Then we moved inside and debated motions and did normal conference things. In those early days of the committee forming, it was natural that the Black Workers Committee, which was first elected about 25 years ago, took the lead on organising the march and rally. So I've been involved with those aspects of the march for close to a quarter of a century.

Being a veteran of the march, one of the things I always look forward to is meeting up and seeing old trade union colleagues. It being November, the weather is not always kind, but that is secondary because there is a collective energy in the atmosphere. You have to be there, you have to feel it in person. The colourful banners add to the vibrancy of the gathering, as do the sounds – the GMB pipe band has always been there, the drumming group SheBoom too. So there's a rhythm.

One of the uplifting constants is the solidarity on the march you feel from the public you pass. There is a celebratory atmosphere, so much positivity coming out of what was in essence a march to counter negativity and hatred.

The far right continue with their efforts, their smears and misinformation, whether it's on migrants or immigration or Islamophobia, so it is vitally important we continue to re-educate everyone. That can be as simple as setting the facts straight. For as long as there has been history, there has been migration and migrants and one of the things the far right latched on to is refugees and asylum seekers. Actually, though, giving people refuge and asylum is one of the most humane things a nation can do. The rally has that message too.

I feel so much pride when I tell people that the St Andrew's Day March and Rally is the only trade union-led annual anti-racism event in the UK. It matters because as long as there are far right organisations seeking power and influence, and as long as there is discrimination against and disadvantage for black people, whether it is direct or systematic, then the trade union movement do need to be there sending out this consistent underlying message.

The far right are creative in how they reinvent themselves. Whether it's the National Front, who used to taunt me when I was a schoolboy, whether it's the BNP, or the Scottish Defence League – while the underlying reason for the march remains challenging racism and fascism, the source of that is ever-changing. We need to remain vigilant.

The things that people march for manifest themselves in different ways. Recent developments have underlined that race equality struggles that are manifested in the legacy of slavery and colonialism are continuing. Recently, George Floyd's murder, and closer to home the murder of Surjit Singh Chhokar and Sheku Bayoh's death in police custody – all of these recent struggles mean that the St Andrew's Day March is more relevant than ever.

There is a quote by Professor Sir Geoff Palmer. 'We can't change the past, but we can change the consequences of the past for the better.' The St Andrew's Day March is all about changing the consequences of the past for the better.

We need to make sure that the march and rally continue as an integral part of the STUC's work. Opposing racism and fascism is a trade union tradition, and it takes persistence, which is probably why we've been marching for a quarter of a century.

Solidarity with Chile

Sonia Leal

When General Pinochet overthrew Chile's socialist government in 1973 and established a dictatorship, five-year-old Sonia's father was imprisoned and tortured for being a trade unionist and a member of the Communist Party. The family later fled Chile with the help of fellow trade unionists, eventually settling in Fife.

INITIALLY WE MOVED to Argentina because my parents didn't want to go far from home. Then there was a coup d'état there, so we had to leave because that was a really aggressive dictatorship as well. Not only were they killing their own people, but they were killing Chileans on sight.

Under the hospice of the United Nations my family became part of a resettlement programme arriving in the UK – my parents, me, my three siblings – in 1977, when I was six. We initially went to an exiles' hotel in Shepherd's Bush in London, and from there we were adopted by the National Union of Mineworkers (NUM) who found us a home in Scotland.

This was as a result of the working groups that had been set up by British volunteers and activists directly after what happened in Chile. There was the Chile Solidarity Campaign, the Chile Committee for Human Rights, and the Chile Defence Committee, which was based in Glasgow. A lot of these organisations were created by trade unionists, church groups and members of left wing political parties united in helping Chilean families who were coming over.

Ours was one of 200 to 300 families who ended up in Scotland. We went to Fife, to live in Cowdenbeath and we had the most amazing welcome. We arrived on May 1st – I don't know whether that was coincidental or not. We got the train to Edinburgh and a bus to Cowdenbeath and we didn't know anything about Scotland. We were learning English back in Chile and Argentina at school, but all we knew about was of England and double decker buses and the Queen!

There was a young voluntary worker in Shepherd's Bush called Helen, aged about 19, and she told us that Scotland was the land of giants, and that the men all had red hair and were so fierce that they could wear skirts and nobody would say anything about it! When we arrived, I remember getting off the bus and there was a pipe band full of men wearing kilts. It was the miners' pipe band because it was May 1st. They piped us all the way through the village to the house and that house was just so beautiful.

My mum and dad couldn't speak any English and the wife of one of the trade union leaders motioned to my mum to open the door with the key. We went inside and every single room was filled with things the whole village had donated. This was when the miners had started going on package holidays to Spain and they'd come back with straw donkeys and flamenco dolls. And so every single windowsill had flamenco dolls on it! There was a straw donkey in every room. Every bed had 10 to 15 blankets on it. They had given so much coal that in the back garden there was this mountain right up to the first-floor window, so that we wouldn't be cold.

The first Christmas we spent there, we came downstairs and you could not see the floor of the sitting room for presents that they had given us. I can't think of a warmer welcome than that. It still makes me very emotional.

There were two old miners who had fought in the Spanish Civil War. They were so lovely. One of them, Ben, had a steel plate in his head and fingers that had been shot off in Spain. He would sing Spanish rebel songs and I always remember them singing to us with their left fist clenched and held up in solidarity. That was their way of communicating with us. The belief that these people had in international solidarity meant that they felt so in tune with us and the Chilean people's plight, and to be able to help us in this manner was so heart-warming.

We all knew the story of East Kilbride and the Rolls-Royce workers, and so did the Chileans back in Chile. We knew that people who were in prison at the time in Chile knew that there was this place called Scotland where there were workers who had done this amazing thing. Those workers had received the engines from the jets that were used to bomb the Chilean parliament on September 11th 1973. They had been sent over to East Kilbride for refurbishment and the shop steward found out where they were from, and he blacked them, which meant no-one was allowed to touch them as they'd been used to bring down the socialist government and the subsequent horror the fascist dictatorship imposed on the Chilean people and mostly trade unionists.

For five years nobody touched them. They were worth a lot of money to Pinochet and the engines became a symbol, particularly in Chile and to Chilean exiles, of international solidarity. It is amazing that people would risk their jobs to help the people of Chile. They risked a lot – they were also threatened by the Chilean military dictatorship, absolute heroes!

There were also dockers who refused to work on Chilean ships that were coming in, in Liverpool, Newcastle, Rosyth and Glasgow. Dockworkers in Newhaven, Liverpool and Hull boycotted handling goods coming in from Chile. There was a decision made by 600 unemployed Liverpool dockworkers to forgo work on freight bound to Chile. In hard times in Britain, they gave up their work to send a message to Chile.

Within the first five years of the Chile Solidarity Campaign, 30 of the national trade unions had affiliated. The unions did an amazing job. The STUC were a big part of that.

That welcome ensured that our family was made to feel part of Scotland and therefore our place in our communities. We took part in the miners' strike, we did loads of campaigning, fundraising, working in the soup kitchens and at times stood with the miners on their picket lines. We are all trade unionists and campaigners to this day. Both my parents were really active in their respective trade unions with my dad setting up his own union called the Latin American Workers Union now representing thousands of workers in London particularly migrant workers and cleaners. I work in a trade union, my sister is an award-winning community activist, and both my brothers have been heavily involved in the arts and music movement both here in Scotland and down south. We have given back a thousandfold because the Scottish miners instilled in us from a really early age that this was our home.

I was a kid at the time when all this happened and even now as a grown woman it saddens me to remember what we lost and what we gained in exile. The trade unions played a big part in our lives then and now need to step up their fight against the hostile environment created by the Tory government against asylum seekers. I feel their plight is much harder than ours; the policies against asylum seekers are abhorrent. Back then, in the '70s, trade unionists took direct action and got their hands dirty when needed – maybe it's time for some proper grass roots organising again!

Union learning and growth in the taxi trade

Stevie Grant

After being made redundant from non-unionised employment in the scientific sector, Stevie became a taxi driver. He later joined Unite, became a rep, helped grow his branch exponentially and developed an important learning tool for colleagues.

I CAME INTO the taxi trade in 2010 wanting to be my own boss. I soon found out that there was a lot wrong in the trade, and that drivers were poorly represented and at the mercy of the licensing authorities as far as rules and regulations were concerned. Deciding what fares we could charge, deciding what vehicle types we could have – all these things were heavily regulated and we didn't seem to have any real trade union representation. That was when I decided to get involved.

It's a job of isolation where workers don't know much about what's going on outside their cab. They're not particularly up to speed on the machinations of the trade outwith what they're doing day to day. We've tried to change that over the past few years and we have grown the branch significantly, from around 50 when we started to 500 now. We've used social media a lot to try and engage the trade and get drivers to fight for their rights.

Members come to us for a mix of reasons. Sometimes they'll fall foul of the rules and regulations – they might have over-ranked on a rank and been pulled in front of the licensing committee, or their badge has expired and they want help getting it renewed. The big thing we represent our members on is the tariff. Glasgow City Council employ a professor to independently look at the tariff and come up with an increase or no increase. We're involved in tariff negotiations if we don't agree with what they propose.

As a trade unionist in the taxi business, the two Covid years were the busiest we'd had. We spent the majority of the time fighting the Scottish Government for proper support. Throughout the pandemic, we were left out because the business support was for fixed premises. They didn't recognise that taxi drivers out there had taxi loans that meant they had to pay hundreds of pounds a month for their vehicles. We fought hard for support and we won limited support. Glasgow taxi drivers received £4,000 in total from the Scottish Government – way below what fixed premises received. It was a really tough time.

I'm now a tutor on the SVQ for Glasgow taxi drivers. We felt that there had been a lowering of standards across the trade, that it had been in decline for a while. There was a feeling of 'We're just taxi drivers, it's not rocket science', when in fact there's a lot more to it than that. You need communication skills, you need to be literate, you need to be numerate. You can be a bad taxi driver, you can be a very good taxi driver. We saw that there needed to be a raising of standards, and for people in the trade to invest in the trade and appreciate the job they're doing and the importance of it.

That spurred us on to getting the council to put in qualifications, which they have done. It's a varied course, the SVQ. There are nine modules in total covering things like vehicle maintenance, safety, safely transporting people, transporting disabled passengers and licensing regulations. It's all important stuff that drivers weren't always aware of.

The feedback from drivers suggests that doing the qualifications has been really worthwhile. There are so many learning opportunities as a trade unionist, and they see that now. There is lifelong learning through the STUC and Unite if they want to do it.

Justice for Colombia

Susan Quinn

Early in the winter of 2020, teacher Susan was part of a trade union delegation that visited Colombia. It increased her sense of internationalism, something central to trade unionists across many years.

A CHARITY, JUSTICE for Colombia, was established in 2002 by the British trade union movement to support Colombian society at large in their struggle with human rights, labour rights, peace and social justice. It still continues to be supported by the wider union movement in Britain. Their main work now is around challenging what is happening in Colombia following the peace agreement of 2016.

Each year since 2016, they have organised this verification mission – a UN-linked expedition to monitor the peace process and its implementation. The trade unions and the TUC and STUC put people forward for that alongside other attendees from politics and charity.

In February 2020, the EIS, my union, were offered a place to be part of that year's mission and I was selected. It was a professional learning opportunity for me, I was so fortunate. It has changed me in terms of my international outlook. I always read the newsletters and gave my donations but never really understood what was going on at more than a surface level.

It is an incredible, astonishing country from what I saw – the trips are controlled. There is a sense of anger that one side put down their weapons and came to a peace agreement, and the other didn't. That one side has done all that they can to bring peace but actually they continue to see growing numbers of their people murdered by government-backed paramilitaries. There is a real frustration that you continue to see that, having seen what the people want to achieve, and having seen what happens to people who speak out against the government.

One of the most impactful parts was meeting with the teachers' trade union. They were talking about their members, ordinary teachers, who were having their lives threatened just for doing their jobs. How can that be right? How can that be acceptable? How can that be something that the world at large isn't challenging more? Teachers are seen as a threat to the government as they are educating young people in peace and peace doesn't suit particular wings of politicians.

The trip was in two parts. In the first part we were based in Bogotá and we were meeting with politicians and other trade unionists. We met with the UN people too. That was a lot about hearing the evidence of what had been done since the last visit to take forward peace, and the challenges that were being faced. So a lot of sitting in rooms, challenging each other, asking questions.

In the second part, there were visits to the countryside to meet with people in communities who were putting peace into practice. That's when you see that these are just people trying to live their lives in a way that is very challenging. We saw a community that had managed to gather the tiny bit of land they were given in the peace process and were going to build their own fish farm. It was good to hear women coming forward to ensure that they had a place within it all.

Similarly, another community in a different situation talked about the challenges they face. The way that the land had been parcelled up out of the peace deal – this group didn't own their land and there was always a worry that they were going to get put off it, that paramilitaries would come and take it. All they were trying to do was raise and educate their children and live in peace.

One of the colleagues there was from Northern Ireland. She likened it to the peace process there, especially when one of the political leaders talked about how factions of his side – on the side of peace – had started to talk about taking up arms again. It really touched her, having gone through that kind of thing.

We had trade unionists with us from the UK and Ireland, Italy, Denmark and elsewhere. A really international group.

Understanding as a trade union movement that we always continue to struggle for the things we do in our own countries, but that there is a world out there and people at a different end of that struggle is very important. It's within us all to provide support, in a whole different set of ways, not just money. It's about seeing them and hearing them and taking their messages back to our parts of the world. It's the right thing to do.

Solidarity visit to Bhopal

Tony Sneddon

Tony is a member of the STUC Disabled Workers' Committee. Thirty years after the 1984 Bhopal disaster, he was part of an STUC delegation to the site. They were there with trade unionists from across the world to show solidarity and demand justice for former workers.

I BELONG TO a mining town, Cowdenbeath. My dad was a miner and he was killed in the pits. The miners' strike and the support from the village for the NUM was instilled in me, as was the anger that went with it. When I joined the Post Office in 1974, that was that, I signed up.

Back in 1984 at a chemical plant in Bhopal, there was a leak of toxic gas that took all the air out of the atmosphere. A large number of people were killed – many, many thousands – or left disabled. It was probably the worst industrial disaster in history.

I heard at a trade union meeting that there was a delegation going from Scotland for the 30th anniversary of the disaster. They asked if anybody would be interested in going. You had to find the money and various levels of sponsorship.

There were people from across the world there. We met with fellow trade unionists in Delhi and Mumbai. It was a show of support and solidarity, and a protest against the American owners – Union Carbide – abandoning Bhopal. The company has since been taken over and they deny all liability. They tried to say that sabotage caused the problem. That's never been proven. But this was a chance to show that the world hadn't forgotten about the victims, and show that workers from other places cared about workers from Bhopal. We carried a banner that said: Scottish Trade Unions – Solidarity With Bhopal.

Some called Bhopal 'a prayer for rain', because they reckon if it had rained, it would have tamed the chemicals down. But as it stood it took all the oxygen so people couldn't breathe. Official figures say 20,000 died. The Americans just walked away. They have a lot to answer for. It now gets used as a playground by children and it is toxic. There is cyanide and all sorts of chemicals there. There are still toxins in the water system surrounding it. It's just rusting away. The company should have had the honesty to decommission the plant and make it safe.

When you see children using the disaster site as a playpark, it's just unbelievable. We were going to get a tour of the site but the Indian government banned anybody from going in because it was a political hot potato, especially with all this interest around the 30th anniversary. They had guards on the gates.

The Scottish Friends of Bhopal support a clinic there, we visited that. They do a mixture of herbal and western medicine, especially to help women who have problems resulting from the pollution after the disaster. We also went to a cinema to see the Martin Sheen film, *Bhopal: A Prayer For Rain*, and some of the survivors were there with us. And there was a museum about it all, converted from a flat in a new build block. In there, we saw a woman crying – she'd seen the child's coat she'd donated, which had belonged to her one-year-old who died. That was heart breaking. There were so many photos of people who died and who'd been turned blind. It was beyond comprehension.

Going there and seeing that, it reconnects you with what's happening to workers across the world. It was a very emotional journey and I have nothing but respect for the people still trying to get justice.

PART 4

The Struggle Continues

THE STUC IS 125 years old and its work will never be done. While workers anywhere face ill-treatment and injustice, it and its member unions will be there. The end of one victory is the beginning of the next one. The issues change but the principles stay the same: together, wrongs are righted and lives improved, here and everywhere. This third section reveals present battles, anticipates labours to come and identifies the next causes for the movement to win. These are the triumphs that trade unionists are working for now and will be in the decades that follow this one.

Here are old, legacy dangers to new workers, hangover struggles still to be overcome and fresh equalities to secure. There are stories of reacting during a pandemic and winning a better aftermath once that ill wind blows through. Others make clear that the protections gained by trade unionists in the last century need now to be refreshed and gained again by the employees of this one. Past lessons and inspirations can help the gig worker in this precarious realm.

Perhaps the flag now is red *and* green. Because here too are words from the trade unionists who may well be active when the STUC strikes 150 and even 175, and they brim with environmental concern. Such causes have aligned and their proponents united. They have a planet to save justly.

These are the stories of what might happen next. Many more victories await.

Pardon for miners
Alex Bennett

Alex became a miner in 1962, aged 15. His father had also been a collier and took part in the 1926 miners' strike. Becoming a trade unionist was a natural progression for Alex, and today he remains committed to righting the wrongs done to his comrades during the 1984 strike.

IN 1969, THERE was an unofficial miners' strike in Scotland on wages. That's the year I got married and moved to Danderhall and began working in the nearby pit, Monktonhall. I was involved with picketing in this unofficial strike. We went back to work without an agreement. Then there was a ballot for a strike in 1972 and I became very much involved in that. Two years later, there was another strike and the miners actually brought down the Heath government and replaced it with a Labour government, which made a big difference to the coal industry at that time. You could see the differences in terms of wages and conditions – people started going on holiday abroad, whereas before it was Butlin's or Blackpool!

Round about the end of the 1970s, I was Vice-chair of the NUM Committee at the pit, and the Chairman, Jimmy Sneddon, was coming up for retirement. So I decided to stand for chairmanship, and Jimmy helped me with that, and I became Chair.

In 1983, Monktonhall went on strike for nine weeks, when a director, Albert Wheeler, who was a pure bastard, stopped the development of the major seam there and the men walked off the job. Then there was a national ballot for an over-time ban, which we took part in. Then in '84, the miners walked off.

Monktonhall was a very productive pit. In 1969, it broke the European production record for its seam height. But it had a militant trade union leadership. Mostly, they were from the Labour left and the British Communist Party, and that's what they were out to destroy, not the industry.

During the '84 strike, I was on the picket line at Bilston Glen Colliery. You were allowed six official pickets at the gates, and I was asked to go there and speak to the men who were still going in to work and to some lorry drivers. When I was there, the police just grabbed me and I got taken to the police station in Dalkeith, where I was fingerprinted and photographed. They were trying to make out that I was inciting a riot, which they were never gonna make stick.

Because of a big push against miners then – June '84, the same time as Orgreave – there was a complete change and all the local policemen, who drank in the same places as us and who we knew, were taken off the frontline and the police that were put on the picket lines were total strangers. They had no connections with the local communities.

I got transferred to the High Street police station in Edinburgh, where I was charged with a breach of the peace as they couldn't make the rioting stick. I appeared in court on December 20th and at the beginning of January 1985, I was found guilty and fined £100. Then I got my P60 through the post, saying I was summarily dismissed. No explanation, no interviews, which we were entitled to. They refused to meet with the union to discuss it and the union was forced to apply for employment tribunals for unfair dismissal. That was for all of us that this had happened to, and there were many – the sackings that took place in Scotland were proportionally the biggest in Britain. About 50 men from my pit alone were sacked. There weren't that many in the whole of South Wales.

The Coal Board had a very weak case, because they'd never interviewed anybody before dismissing them. Some men were taken back, but I never got my job back. I should've got £27,000 redundancy money, which was a lot in 1985. But I got £12,000 compensation from the Employment Tribunal instead.

But it was the blacklisting that really hurt, the trying to get a job. They were electrifying the railways from London to Aberdeen and their base was not far from here, down in Millerhill. I applied for a job and didn't even get an interview. Some of the boys that worked there told me: 'Alex, you didn't get an interview because they didn't want to employ striking miners.'

The blacklisting went on for three years and was the hardest bit. My daughter Lynn was 15, and she'd been going to Hillend with school, learning to ski. The school was taking them to the Alps for a skiing trip. Normally I would've been OK to pay for that – you're delighted to see your daughter do something like that. But I had to tell her that I couldn't afford it. Her words to me were, 'Dad, it's OK, because my two pals, their fathers are in the same boat as you. They're miners, so we understand what it's all about.' Then finally, Amco, a Yorkshire company, were doing contract work in the Scottish coalfield and my old union contacts phoned me and set me up some work with them, driving tunnels. So I got back to earning money again, but I still didn't forget what we went through.

We still want justice for that dismissal in the form of a Pardon for Miners, and I hope the Scottish Parliament deliver it. Up to now, they've said they will – I was part of the team that met with them – but haven't delivered. To try and get that, we've had a lot of meetings with lawyers and politicians. We've also all got together as ex-miners, including a big meeting in the National Mining Museum in Newtongrange which miners from across Scotland attended. We all had the same point of view: all we want is justice and a pardon.

The man who has driven much of this campaign for a pardon is the ex-Labour MSP Neil Findlay. There have been other political supporters in favour of us getting a pardon too. We reckon if we get it here, and we are always in touch with our comrades in Durham, Yorkshire and elsewhere, then we could get an inquiry into Orgreave. What happened there was disgusting, and nobody was charged, and that stinks of corruption. Just look at Hillsborough. We're still fighting for justice there. We've got unity with miners across the UK.

There's still a lot of work to do. A lot of things still aren't right. We want justice, and down the line perhaps we'll be entitled to lost wages and lost pension rights. But for now, we just want justice through the Pardon; that has got to be the priority. It's an ongoing fight. There is still a job for retired miners to do.

Safe Home campaign

Caitlin Lee

As a child, Caitlin was fascinated by the political and trade union messages of her dad's musical choices in the car. Now in her mid-20s and a bartender in a hotel, she is Chair of Unite's Glasgow Hospitality Branch.

IN JUNE 2020, my workplace made the decision to make 63 per cent of the workforce redundant. We were actually the lucky ones because in another of their hotels nearby, they made 95 per cent redundant. There was outrage and people didn't know what to do. That happened on a Monday, and by the Wednesday I'd chaired a call of about 70 colleagues, telling them they needed to join the union and then what we needed to demand. I threw myself into it.

I was elected the representative of my 'department' and with Unite put alternatives to redundancy forward. I communicated the situation on social media too. I asked a few questions which the employer answered but then backtracked on. For instance, I asked if I could be represented by my trade union organiser in meetings and was told 'Yes.' Then everyone got a mass email a month later saying 'You do not have any legal requirement to be represented.' So I had to do things like circulate that original answer I'd had. It wasn't inspiring, uplifting trade unionism; it was grabbing what you could. I did enjoy being able to stand up to the bosses and demand more, and that was because I knew I had someone at my back. Having the collective behind you empowers you. Being able to be loud and call out my employer and know I was making a difference was brilliant.

I managed to keep my job but many others didn't so that was obviously difficult. We went into the second lockdown in January 2021 and we restarted the Glasgow Hospitality Branch. That's when I stood to be Chair, even though I'd never done anything like that before. We're not a workplace branch – we're Glasgow Hospitality and Services, so we look at issues that affect workers across the city. That gives us the benefit of having members sprawled throughout different bars and hotels. We have over 2,000 members, all dotted about, which gives us a good geographic spread. It means as well as workplace issues, we look more widely at societal issues. Improving society is an important element of our branch.

That all chimed with the Safe Home campaign. It was begun by the STUC's Better Than Zero campaign a few years ago, and driven on by Cineworld workers. They had cut out clippings about sexual assaults in the city and handed them out to show how much they needed to be provided with free safe transport to get them home after night shifts, which was the key aim of Safe Home. We also have Safe Home within our Unite Hospitality Charter, which has nine key demands for a workplace to adopt to become a better place to work.

Getting home safely was already an issue before the pandemic, but back then lots of us used to go for drinks after work and then go home together. But that social element of working stopped, and we noticed how hard it was to get home. There were now no night buses.

In March 2021, Sarah Everard was murdered by a police officer while walking home. We reflected on that. We opened our branch meeting that month with that topic. The main thing that came from that apart from anger was 'That could've been me.' We began to talk about the risks we faced in hospitality, especially as women. We talked about the sexual harassment that occurs, and what we face when we have to walk home. What we deal with on a daily basis. We looked at our industry as one where this was allowed to happen, and we started to talk about what we needed to do to combat it.

There was a lot of reflection and anger and discussion over what to do. We surveyed our members and the stats that came back – well it was hard to read. There was a resounding lack of confidence in the police's ability to deal with these things, and a resounding amount of people who had been sexually assaulted. People felt very unsafe getting home. We made videos on the back of that, demanding change.

Unite then took on what we were doing and made it nationwide. A previous campaign called Not on the Menu was relaunched. We began to come up with tangible demands – what can we do about this as a branch. It was things that an employer should have been doing; we realised we *should* be getting transported home. There was a feeling of 'Why isn't this happening?' We put our personal experiences together too. For instance, once Covid restrictions were eased and bars could open later I was having to pay for my taxis home as there was no public transport at night. I dreaded that restriction change as I couldn't get the last bus anymore. There was dread about getting home once we'd lost the safety net of finishing earlier.

At the end of July 2021, I was supposed to be working until 1am. I'd raised the issue with my employer about having to pay for my own transport home and about the unsafe nature of working late. I was told that's just the reality of working in hospitality. I had a heated argument with my manager, and said I didn't think I should have the financial burden of getting home. My wage is £9 an hour. A taxi is at least an hour and a half's wages. One cocktail in my workplace is an hour's wages. For me it's a huge thing, for a company it's nothing. The solution was that I finished at midnight and got the last bus. They just would not pay.

The last bus didn't arrive, as they often don't. I walked through the city centre hoping a taxi would come towards me. That didn't happen because I was sexually assaulted on the street by a complete stranger. The only reason I was there was because I was trying to get home from work. The only reason I then got home safely that night was because I was in a police car.

The aftermath, beyond the personal emotional horror, was that my employer was horrific. I put a grievance in and a demand that they recognise what happened to me and make sure it never happened again by paying for taxis home. They made the decision not to do that and stated that an employer's duty of care does not extend beyond the workplace. They're a huge employer across the world and we need to get them to accept they do have a duty of care. And that does entail, when there's no transport, getting people home safely.

The Safe Home campaign also looks beyond employers. It calls out the licensing boards because their whole focus is on the customer and not the worker. Priority needs to be on both customer *and* staff safety. At busy times like Christmas, all licences can be extended by an hour. If hours are being extended just so places can make more profit like this, then people need to be getting home safely. We're building a collective of workers so together we feel the confidence to demand these things.

There have been successes so far. East Dunbartonshire Council have made Safe Home a licensing policy – anyone who works past midnight, their employer has to get them home. So it is possible. We will keep going and we will get there.

Working together for climate justice
Catrina Randall

Catrina works for Friends of the Earth Scotland and has seen what climate activists and trade unionists working together can achieve. Her union awareness sprang from family lore: legend has it that her great-grandmother unionised workers in London's pickle factories.

MEMBERS OF FRIENDS of the Earth Scotland (FOES) and the climate movement decided to join trade union picket lines during COP26 (UN Climate Change Conference, held in Glasgow in 2021) because we wanted to show solidarity with the workers. The bottom line was that they deserved better working conditions and good wages. They were workers taking action in vital services like cleansing, and on the railways, which we obviously need in our transition to a more sustainable way of life. We need good public transport, we need good waste systems and within those systems the workers need to be treated fairly and have good working conditions.

Beyond that, it was also that we know we are fighting the same struggle. We know that climate justice *is* workers' rights, climate change is an issue that is not just about the natural world, but is a political and social issue as well. It's the same economic system that is exploiting and extracting the natural world that is exploiting and extracting from workers. We need to change our economic system, and the best ways we have to combat capitalism and the exploitation of people is strong trade unionism.

Our interests are aligned, and we wanted to show up and show solidarity. There has been a false binary between the labour movement and the climate movement. It has quite often been presented as climate activists versus workers. Actually, they are often the same people – climate activists are workers, are working class, especially young people precariously employed. They are interested in the environment and are interested in joining trade unions. They see it as part and parcel of the same thing. Realising we are the same people having the same fight and bringing those things together is important. It is exciting that that is becoming more explicit.

At COP26, a lot of folk were aware the strikes were happening and had been vocal with their support. Then the call came for people to stand on the picket lines. Messages were going out through group chats and across social media. I went to the GMB cleansing workers picket line first, at 7am. We had our signs – 'Climate Movement Supports the Strikers', and 'Climate Justice = Workers' Justice'. There was such heavy policing in Glasgow. People were getting stopped for any sign of being protestors. We had to conceal our placards on the Subway and trains.

We turned up and there were lots of cleansing workers, and a crowd from Friends of the Earth, and Fridays for Future and others. Somebody had brought a sound system, and they started blasting out clubland tunes. Absolute beats. We were dancing outside the cleansing centre. It was incredible. People were welcoming, and everyone was buzzing, and sharing snacks.

Cleansing workers and people from the GMB spoke, and climate activists and international trade unionists, including representatives from Friends of the Earth India talking about the struggles of waste workers there and linking the struggles to climate issues. It felt like such a powerful moment of international solidarity and solidarity across all of these different borders and sectors coming together and making the links between all these issues.

The next one I went to was the RMT picket line at Central Station; that was at 11 at night. A lot of people came to that from all sorts of causes and groups, and of course the railway workers. Again the music started up and the dancing. It was the closest I'd been to a nightclub in two years. Workers rights and dancing in the streets to Abba. Incredible.

There was a sudden sense that this is where real change comes from – not global leaders with their vested interests, sitting inside some sterile hall, but people out here on the streets, building relationships and connections between causes. Learning from each other, building power.

It's important we continue these relationships and for the climate movement to show it wasn't just the opportune moment of COP and a way of furthering our cause. It was about showing that we are serious about standing with trade unionists and standing with workers, and we are going to keep showing up. There's so much to learn from trade unions and their understanding of power and their strategies. I work with Young FOES, and we've started talking with young trade union groups through the STUC about how we can work together and learn. There's so much potential in us working together. And that'll have the people in power running scared.

Protecting black workers in a pandemic

Charmaine Blaize

Alongside being a Service Development Manager with NHS 24, Charmaine is Unison Black Workers' Committee's Education Officer, a union rep and an equalities officer. During the pandemic, she helped identify the disproportionate problems of black workers.

I BECAME A trade unionist when I was back home in Trinidad after graduating from university. My uncles were hardcore activists. My great uncles and uncles were in the equivalent of the STUC in Trinidad. But I was never really active until I came to Scotland.

In April 2020, the website Nursing Notes alarmingly reported that over 100 healthcare staff had died in the early stages of the pandemic, with over 70 per cent of them being black workers. So there we were as black workers facing a pandemic, disproportionately high infection and death rates, and no meaningful response or solutions in sight. We decided that we needed to have a strategic response to identify known risks and provide interventions.

Unison Scotland Black Members Committee commissioned a survey to analyse the experience of black workers as compared to all workers engaged in Covid-19 work across health, social care and local government. We discovered a climate of fear among black workers: fear of speaking up, fear of dying from Covid, fear of infecting family members, fear of no access to PPE and proper equipment, fear of job loss and loss of pay. There was a higher level of fear than with white workers. Black workers found themselves overexposed to the virus and under protected compared to white counterparts. The analysis from that survey was a trigger point for us to try to expose what was happening. We concluded that bad jobs kill. Fair work saves lives.

Unison Scotland shared these results of this survey widely. Within the union, interventions included creating and sharing a Covid Equally Safe Plan, promoting safe work for all, devising a Health and Safety training module with an equalities focus, and we held a webinar that located racism as a public health issue.

The Scottish Government in response developed a safety protocol for PPE for all workers that all employers were supposed to follow. It also formed an Expert Reference Group (ERG) on Covid and Ethnicity to address this. The Scottish Government's *Programme for Scotland 2020–2021: Protecting Scotland, Renewing Scotland* includes recommendations raised by the ERG. Black and Ethnic Minority Infrastructure Scotland (BEMIS) – the national umbrella body supporting the development of the ethnic minorities voluntary sector – is a member of that ERG and invited the Unison Black Workers Committee to partner with them and create an Ethnic Minority Resilience Network. I was asked to Chair that. We did things like support the Eastern Europeans who were working in Aberdeen where there was a big outbreak of Covid and factory workers in that area weren't getting support.

One of the interventions delivered by BEMIS was the use of emergency sustenance fund payments to ensure people from Black and Minority Ethnic (BME) backgrounds could receive vitally needed support and access to food and other supplies regardless of immigration status.

We sent Freedom of Information requests to all health boards asking for the number of staff who have had risk assessments broken down by ethnicity as per the census. We got responses from several health boards but not all, and many of them didn't answer the questions, because one of the flaws with the risk assessment protocol is that it didn't have a feedback system to check employers did what they were supposed to be doing. There was no reporting. We could also see that there was a big cluster of black workers in low paid jobs compared to white workers. They were over-represented in lower pay bandings, and highly under-represented in high bandings. That information was fed back to the Scottish Government – career progression and risk assessment being done or not being done. I spoke at an STUC Congress about all of this.

Pandemics are followed by recessions, further job loss and cuts to public spending, so we will continue to follow-up on compliance to risk assessments to protect workers' safety and rights. As trade unions we need to come together to actively engage with and monitor progress of the Scottish Government's Programme for Scotland, an ambitious plan to deal with many of the systemic and structural issues in the short, medium and long-term. Some interesting features to develop include a measure for racism.

One of the costs of racism is death. The tragic deaths of George Floyd in the United States and close to home Mercy Baguma reminds us of this. For black workers, Covid discriminated due to societal, systemic and structural barriers faced by us. Imagine we can invent a vaccine against the virus in eight months, yet over 400 years have passed and we are yet to find a vaccine for racism. During Covid, the cost of racism has powered movements like Black Lives Matter and opened the hearts and minds of many different people in a positive manner on a global scale.

Black workers can feel isolated in Scotland, and there needs to be more outreach work by unions so they know they are not alone. We have to always raise our voice and not be afraid to speak up.

As activists, we have a captive audience now. There is much work to do, and this is a moment of opportunity for all of us. People are listening compassionately and willing to act. We have one race, the human race, so race equality is everyone's business. We cannot say we are non-racist or we are the least racist: we must strive to be actively anti-racist. We need to do more now. We need to do better now.

Climate and unions at COP26

Coll McCail

Coll, a young climate activist, was galvanised by the Fridays For Future school strikes of 2019. COP26 – the UN Climate Change Conference, held in Glasgow in 2021 – saw him and his fellow activists come together with trade unionists, casting a template for united action.

FRIDAYS FOR FUTURE is the movement which came out of the environmental school strikes that started in Sweden. Since then it's evolved into an international movement in most countries across the world. It still revolves around the idea of schools striking on Fridays, but also as consciousness of climate justice among young people develops, a movement has grown into a broader coalition of young people in the fight for system change.

COP26 was an interesting experience for me. It was a coalition of people coming together – trade unionists, climate activists, migrants' rights activists, anti-racism activists, tenants' unions – as a broad coalition of causes united under one banner. That was incredible to be a part of, and we made connections that we'll take into the future. That was special because during the pandemic, the idea of solidarity was so constrained – it was a slogan with no physical manifestation. So to come straight from that to COP, where you could turn up at a picket line and there'd be a huge amount of organisations there and that would be reciprocated at your event, was really special.

You got the sense of this mass movement, this coalition that could make change. That leant into ideas about tactics. For so long every movement was guilty of being isolated in its struggles, and of course that puts us at a disadvantage. We've fought these battles in isolation, but COP didn't feel like that.

One of the things we wanted to do during COP was build a material link between climate and labour that we were guilty of not trying to build in the past. That is important because if you want a just transition to a green climate then there will have to be a united front in the fight for that. Sometimes, there have been perceived tensions between the climate movement and the trade union movement. There is guilt on the side of the climate movement for that – historically, a kind of general apathy and also some had this middle-class attitude towards the more general workers' struggle, plus the targets the climate movement has picked over the last couple of years, they haven't been appropriate, or legitimate targets. They haven't been polluters or decisions makers, they're been working-class people. There's a guilt on our side that that is unfathomably wrong.

So when it looked like there was going to be this massive industrial front organising in Glasgow ahead of COP – Caledonian Sleeper workers, ScotRail workers, the refuse workers all on strike – we saw an opportunity to get more involved with that and to build those links. That's how we ended up at an RMT picket line at Glasgow Central Station. Caledonian Sleeper workers – their fight is our fight. Climate justice means workers' justice. It means fair pay, it means workers' rights. So we went to show our support. It was an incredible night. The flags, the singing, the dancing the slosh.

COP is designed to be this alienating experience for 'real people'. Just look at some of the things that happened in Glasgow – tenants turfed out of their homes, free travel cards for only delegates, limousines blocking roads, women forced to walk dangerous routes at night because delegates were in Kelvingrove – even in the face of all of that, there was this boundless solidarity. That was surprising, which makes it all the more special.

I hope we'll keep those connections going because I think they were really valuable. As we go forward, there has to be one united coalition movement that makes the case for a radical green deal that is explicitly anti-capitalist and that can galvanise people. That has to convene workers and young people. The roots for that were laid during COP.

Worker safety during Covid
Deborah Vaile

Deborah is a library assistant at the Royal Botanic Garden Edinburgh. She has been a rep for 10 years and a health and safety rep for five. During the Covid pandemic, health and safety reps faced new challenges in trying to protect their members through an uncertain and tense time.

WHEN IT SEEMED obvious that Covid was coming and was going to affect things, we had to get organised quickly. First we had to organise how the horticulture workers could safely stay at work, because of course they'd be needed to keep the plants alive. We got them onto a safe rota system of three days on, three days off.

The Visitor Welcome Team were understandably very nervous up to the beginning of lockdown, having to face the public but not knowing how safe it was. About 75 per cent of staff were furloughed. The management included me in their planning meetings at that stage, so I was able to communicate what was happening to members.

During lockdown, it was harder to get information from management, but we told members what we could. The members seemed to be looking to us for information rather than management. It's a challenge to get information and to be consulted, so you just have to keep trying. It was us that raised the issue of ventilation as well, and it took a while for them to understand how important it was. Now they include it in their planning. Members often remind me that it was the union that made that happen.

Externally, there was a TUC forum for all reps, split into different sections and including a health and safety group. Reps for all unions post queries and other reps reply and give advice. That's been really good for me during Covid. There are some really good reps on there.

There was a lot of anxiety when we reopened too. We were the first visitor attraction to reopen in Edinburgh. The visitor welcome team were understandably anxious. There has also been an increase in aggression from visitors, mainly when the welcome team have to enforce Covid regulations. It was the same across other heritage venues – frontline staff getting grief. They get hit the most and are the lowest paid. We as reps had to make sure everything that could be done was done to protect them. It has been a constant battle.

Unionising produce workers
Derek Mitchell

While employed in the fresh produce industry, Derek helped win union recognition and improve other conditions having become a rep for USDAW. His union pedigree came from his parents, both Timex workers involved in the famous actions at their Dundee factory.

BEING IN A union is not just about workplace protection. It's about everything they offer – they are there for the workers, not the company. A lot of workplaces take the piss out of their workers, and we can't stand for that. Fundamentally, the workers should be treated fairly in the workplace. That's a strong passion of mine.

When I joined my workplace about 20 years ago we were standing outside the factory trying to get recognition for USDAW in the workplace, because until then they wouldn't give us that. It was a sort of picket line trying to push for that agreement. We finally got that. That was an important moment.

The money is a big factor in my industry. It's the lowest paid part of the food manufacturing sector in the UK. The conditions of some factories are horrible, an absolute joke. Things need to change for the better in this sector.

I work across the sector for the union now. It's a cold and wet working environment, and that's made worse by people being treated unfairly. Say you have to take a day off sick – you're pulled in for an absence review for having one day off, regardless of the fact that your attendance has been perfect for the last six months. Things like that.

We're like the backroom staff, unseen. People have only started thinking about us much through 2021, 2022 with the problems that have led to empty shelves. We have to show how critical we are in the food supply chain – if it wasn't for us, people wouldn't eat, and now they were seeing that. We would like that to be reflected in our working conditions.

We do manage as trade unionists to get wins. A few years ago, we won paid breaks, which was a massive thing for us. We got shift allowance at the same time, that was big too. Recently, we won a pay increase too. They're the kind of things you're most proud of as a trade unionist – when you stand together as a unit and you've got something you've asked for or you've stopped something negative the company is trying to implement. It's about teamwork, and about being strong and tight for each other.

A unique LGBT+ network
Eilidh Milliken

Hospital pharmacist Eilidh is a member of the Pharmacists' Defence Association. Here Eilidh outlines firstly the campaigning work of their long-running National Association of Women Pharmacists, and then the role of a unique LGBT+ group for fellow union members.

THE NATIONAL ASSOCIATION of Women Pharmacists (NAWP) has been around since 1905. It was founded in London when a group of female pharmacists came together in a time when it was a male-dominated profession to fight and advocate for equal opportunities for women in pharmacy. Over the years this has developed and grown, and in the last few years has come under the wing of the PDA.

I was elected onto the committee as Honorary Secretary and our committee has grown since then. Now we do a variety of things. We have really come together to create and organise events and factsheets during the pandemic. We get together every few months to come up with ideas of how we can raise awareness of issues relating to women in pharmacy and women's health. For example, we've done factsheets on the menopause, we've held an event on International Women's Day to mark women in leadership and managed to get women from different leadership roles in pharmacy to speak about how they got there and the barriers they faced. NAWP membership is open to all women, that includes transgender women and non-binary people, and if men want to join as allies they are welcome too. It is an intersectional network, organising events for everyone.

We have tried to be active on social media, across different platforms. We produce newsletters with member articles and appear on podcasts. We've also done blogs about domestic violence, and factsheets about breast cancer awareness, cervical screening awareness.

The PDA LGBT+ Network is the first of its kind in pharmacy, and it's something that's very important to a lot of people as a safe, inclusive space for people of different sexualities and genders to come together and speak about different issues that they've faced. We have a WhatsApp group for members for that. The Network created badges for people to wear in the workplace to make patients and healthcare workers aware of what pronouns they use and to show allyship to transgender, gender-queer and gender non-conforming people and to show this is a safe and open space.

This group matters so much because it might appear that we live in an equal society but there are so many micro-aggressions and biases which occur constantly in the workplace for patients and for staff. There are all sort of things that people aren't aware of, so it's nice to be able to come together with a group of fellow professionals who understand it and are ready to stand up to it as a collective and say: 'Well actually no, this is not OK.'

The PDA and other trade unions have a role to play in all of this as they need to understand the barriers faced by LGBT+ people, women, people with ability issues, people of different ethnic backgrounds – that needs to come from the ground up, from the people who face them day to day. So really the PDA's responsibility is to listen and to work with members to understand what needs to be done to help face and challenge these issues, especially if employers for example are discriminating against their staff.

In the world of pharmacy I'd never encountered equality networks before, and it is easy to feel isolated without those connections. It's great that pharmacists are finally stepping up to the fact that certain things in our profession that need challenging.

Changing the music industry

Iona Fyfe

Folksinger Iona joined the Musicians' Union aged 16. Eight years on, she is an active committee member. Here, she charts what union membership has done for artists, and the future changes that they will strive to make.

THE BENEFITS THE Musicians' Union (MU) offered were really good when I joined, as they are now. Instrument insurance and publishing rates that said how much you should be paid, that kind of thing. I once had a contract marked up by the MU's lawyers, and that saved me nearly a year's membership fee immediately. Then when I was older I began to understand the collective action of membership and things like lobbying for improvements. Joining a union is always the right thing to do. It should be second nature to people.

There are quite a few issues that come up a lot. For instance, situations where people's intellectual property has been plagiarised. The main thing for me has been fee collections – if someone's been dragging their heels with paying you, saying 'Okay, I'm going to get the union involved' spurs them into action. There was also an issue a few years ago about venues charging back PRS to artists. That meant there had to be a conversation between them and the MU. And things like venues charging musicians to sell their CDs, even though venues aren't even providing a table or staff. That's another time where we suggest a conversation with the union. A lot of the main issues are about fairness: making sure bands are being paid for their work and pay to play isn't happening, where you have to sell 'x' amount of tickets before you start getting paid.

The union is able to help with those things, and then there are individual gains. Last year, Scottish Rugby Union put out a call for artists to submit their music in a competition. They would then pick a selection of artists to create a Spotify list of, and they would give a performance opportunity at Murrayfield, in return for free tickets for the musician's family and friends. That is not good enough. Murrayfield is a massive stadium with big ticket sales. It was ridiculous to think they could ask for that for free. Very swiftly, people took to social media to say that the SRU should pay the musicians. The MU were included in that and put pressure on, and they u-turned and apologised. It hopefully made similar organisations aware that you can't do that.

There are other things we've raised awareness of. In 2019 I was thinking about the musicians around me that have children, wondering how on earth they managed. A lot of the venues we played in just weren't clean. There were no fridges for breast milk. Some didn't even have a Green Room. No-one was asking for fancy Green Rooms, just basic spaces where you could have privacy and fit a pram or a travel cot. Things that would allow new parents to take their children on tour with them. That's a barrier especially for females who happen to be the care giver a lot of the time, biologically because they have to feed, and it prevents them getting back to work. I had a motion on that accepted unanimously at conference, but then the pandemic hit and obviously no-one toured anyway. So that's one to pick up in the future.

We've also recently started to raise the topic of gender inequality and sexual harassment in the folk and traditional music scene. It's so pervasive. I'm almost desensitised to it now. It goes from micro-aggressions to full out assault. It happens in every genre. The Musicians' Union have had this Code of Conduct which organisations and individuals have signed. Signing means holding yourself to standards and if people don't behave according to them then they go. I've not had anyone in my band be inappropriate, but there have been instances where actually some band leaders have fired musicians because they've investigated incidents.

I hope that my union, and the STUC and others, play a part in raising awareness about this in the future so we can make changes. Perhaps there could be legal support for victims – it's very likely a woman could be charged with libel or defamation if she makes an allegation because she doesn't have legal proof that it happened. That fear stops so many people from speaking out.

Making a stand with Macmerry

Keetah Konstant

As the STUC's 125th year began, bartender Keetah was campaigning for better working conditions and union recognition in the hospitality industry. Colleagues at the Macmerry 300 chain of bars had begun collective action over issues common in that sector.

THE CATALYST FOR the Macmerry 300 campaign came at Christmas 2021 over their dealing with Covid. A lot of people became ill or had to isolate, and it became very apparent how much more the company valued money over us and our health. That was frustrating, and from there people started discussing other issues and we decided to compile a collective grievance with everything that people had been dealing with for the past two years or so.

Various troubling things were raised. People's pensions were being taken from their payslips but not being put into the pension pot. Staff were owing money in tax when they shouldn't have been. There were maintenance issues in all the venues, often dangerous ones. A few venues didn't have proper ventilation during Covid, which is obviously a huge health and safety risk. There were several sexual predators in the company which the owners knew about and did nothing. People were tired of it all.

The collective grievance was the first step, and then we had a meeting with the owners. They haven't done as much as we'd like. It's been a very surface-level response from them. The core issues haven't been dealt with appropriately, which is frustrating. We have had demonstrations and pickets, but we're focusing mainly on the virtual side of campaigning – flyers, social media – to bring attention to our cause.

People are still having to ask for the holiday pay that they are legally entitled to. Ex-staff are being flatly ignored when it comes to that. Staff just aren't being paid what they are owed. That's the first step, because it's a very base, bare minimum ask. That's what we're hoping for, and eventually for them to fix some of the bigger maintenance issues. And then to recognise Unite Hospitality as our union so we can work together in future to create a better workplace for everyone, and to sign the Fair Hospitality Charter so that they are held accountable in future.

I'd really like to see more bar, restaurant and café teams coming together. I don't see why our industry should be the only one that doesn't get that. Our boss claims it is a highly-regulated industry, but it isn't. They can get away with so much. We should be able to have union representation like any other industry. In the wider scheme of things, that's what I'd like to see.

I've been involved with the STUC's Better Than Zero and Young Workers projects since before the Macmerry campaign. They are places for workers to get together and talk about how to achieve this goal of getting more hospitality and retail and other precarious workplaces unionised. We've held workshops and explored the history of trade unions and how to unionise a workplace. We've also gone on walks around town where we go into workplaces and ask them if there are any issues with their workplace, and what would they like to see done. From then on we introduce them to the concept of trade unions – that project is called Workers Reunion.

I feel we have a real opportunity in the hospitality sector to organise in a more radical way than a lot of sectors do because we are so new. It's an opportunity to make real, strong change instead of following the usual service sector model. That's something that's really exciting and I'm hoping that as we grow in the hospitality branches and sector within the union, we can influence other sectors to go back to the more effective tactics and collectivism of the past.

Battling labour casualisation in academia

Lena Wanggren

The university sector employs great numbers of academic staff on a casual, precarious basis. Lena has worked to raise the problems these insecure conditions result in through her research and in her role as a trade union rep with UCU.

THE FIRST THING affecting precarious workers is the state of being in limbo, and never seeing an end in sight, where you are always looking for a job, and you're never sure if they are going to pay you right.

The second thing is insecurity. When you are precarious, this is not just financial, but it goes into every single aspect of your life – you can't plan a family, you can't plan long-term relationships because you don't know if you're going to stay. In academia, because the workplace is so spread out, it might be that next month you'll have to move to another city, or even another country. It is about never being able to put down roots, never being able to fully-engage with your colleagues. Insecurity in all areas of your life.

The third thing precarious work in higher education affects is health. Mental and physical, it is just never-ending. We have low level anxiety continuously about how to pay rent and keep afloat.

There is a real gender aspect to this. Research in 2019 showed that you are more likely to be on a precarious contract if you are a woman than a man, and if you are BAME than if you are a white person.

I meet a lot of casualised, precarious workers in higher education who say that they don't care about their employer but they care about their union. At the moment I have three different employers, so I don't feel at home in any particular workplace but I do feel at home in my union. If you are powerless in your workplace, and you don't have an employee category or an office space and you are not consulted on issues, in your union you can still make a change.

I think precarity affects the quality of the work at the university. Not because me and others don't do our best, but, for example, if you don't have an office, it's difficult to meet students. If you don't have any paid time to meet with students, you either do it for free in a café, or you don't do it. I meet some in the corridor, for instance. So their learning is suffering.

The trade union movement is decades behind. Half of my own colleagues are on precarious contracts. When you speak to most senior colleagues, they have no idea. It's a two-tier system. In other sectors, they can't believe what the university sector is like. Hospitality have known about this problem for a while, but a lot of unions are just so far behind in organising and catching up with what the labour market is like. But for precarious workers, being so short of money and being anxious is just normal.

We have had loads of victories, despite all of this. When I first joined, I organised a network for casualised people and I went to every school in the university. I said 'Hello, you can join the union' because people didn't know. Slowly we got more and more people involved. Now half of our branch committee are casualised workers, which is representative of how things look in terms of contracts. And our union membership has doubled in the last ten years, and I think a lot of those people are casualised people.

In 2013, we campaigned and we had a petition and we got the university to ban Zero Hours contracts. They moved us to guaranteed-hours contacts, which in some ways in practice is like a Zero Hours contract, but it was still a win. We have had so many small wins such as making sure hourly paid staff get paid for marking essays, and paid for training too. Things that didn't happen before. A few years ago, we put in a claim and won an agreement on anti-casualisation, and I believe that's the only collective agreement that we've had at Edinburgh University since UCU formed.

The small wins are good but the bigger win is that people are now aware that casualisation exists in this sector, and that these precarious workers feel they have power. We are making changes for the better all the time.

Action on Asbestos

Phyllis Craig

Since graduating with a law degree more than 25 years ago, Phyllis has worked for the charity Action on Asbestos. Working hand-in-hand with the STUC and trade unions, she has battled for the rights of workers suffering with asbestos-related conditions.

WHEN I JOINED Clydeside Action on Asbestos as it was called then, the management committee were very much trade union orientated. They were union members, mostly T&G branch 7/162 – all the laggers. These men all had asbestos-related conditions but were proactive in their fight for justice with the unions and with the STUC. That's how I became involved with the STUC – it was something so important to our clients, having STUC and union support.

Our clients had been affected by asbestos exposure through no fault of their own. They had been exposed to asbestos negligently and the union people were passionate about trying to make workplaces much safer. Over the years we have had so many campaigns, all of which were supported by the unions and this has only been because there have been so many injustices placed on people who suffer an asbestos condition.

The people who we represent are ill because of the negligence of others – the companies who knew the dangers of asbestos exposure, but profit seemed to come first. It cost thousands of lives and caused many to be severely debilitated in later years. Seeing these families every day is what motivates me and the people who work here. During my period of employment here and when fighting each campaign, the unions were always so supportive. Our charity would combine our efforts with all of the unions to ensure that people who were going out every day to work were going to be working in a safe environment and treated with the respect they should be.

When I started it was men who had worked in the shipyards – laggers, joiners, plumbers, electricians, you name it. But as time went on, we started to see a shift from the shipbuilding industry into construction – people who worked in maintenance in hospitals and people who worked in schools. All public buildings where asbestos was contained, really.

We initiate campaigns with the support of the unions to get MSPs to try and face these injustices that are being put upon these men and women. And we try and remedy it so that they can get compensation. We have fought for their compensation even when they were dying.

We will do anything that has to be done. It might be lobbying MSPs, especially to get over this myth that asbestos conditions are a thing of the past, because that's not true. We had 750 newly diagnosed cases in 2020. People always believe that because it was some time ago, and because there are no shipyards now, there are no conditions. But the latency period is between 15 and 30 years, so it means that someone who was exposed 20 to 30 years ago can only be diagnosed with a terminal or severely debilitating disease now. We have to make sure that things are in place. People who were left debilitated have needed the force of the unions and the way they stand their ground. It is a continuous fight for the rights of these workers.

There have been various campaigns – the campaign for the right of relatives to damages, for instance. We campaigned to the Scottish Parliament, we went before the Justice Committee and we argued our point, and we were successful. In 2007, the Relatives' Damages Act came into force. That meant that the affected person could take their damages in life but their family and their dependents could also, following their death, go and pursue damages for their own loss and their grief. Before that, a person dying of mesothelioma had to choose whether to take their compensation in life and leave nothing for their relatives, or to take nothing and hope those relatives would get something when they passed away. The unions were so supportive of that campaign and backed everything that we did.

Another thing has been to raise awareness of women with mesothelioma and asbestos-related conditions. People always think: 'Oh they must have got it from washing their husband's overalls.' We have to get away from that myth because women always worked. If it is recorded that it is someone's secondary exposure because of someone's overalls they were washing, then that's detrimental in the pursuit of civil damages.

There is also an increase in young female teachers being diagnosed with mesothelioma. That's because it is present in schools. There are more than 1,600 schools in Scotland that contain asbestos. If you have an older school, a lorry going by that shakes the building even just slightly releases the fibres. So children and young teachers are exposed to asbestos every day. We are raising that a lot with the collaboration of unions.

Asbestos doesn't care about class or ethnicity. We have to make people realise that this is going to cause deaths in the future. We are standing up with the unions now and saying, 'Look, there has got to be something done.' The unions are fighting hard for that.

Asda equal pay

Rose Theresa Skillin

In 2016, Asda workers like Rose Theresa were delighted to hear a tribunal agree with their equal pay claim, brought by GMB. The case has since been upheld in the Court of Appeal and the Supreme Court. Rose Theresa and others are battling on until equality is achieved.

WHEN I WAS young, I worked in a bookies next door to Ravenscraig steelworks. We used to take the workers food during the big strikes, and they used to come in to get warmed up as it was so cold on the picket line. We'd chat and I used to ask them all about it. I've always been political – anti-poll tax and anti-racism demonstrations, things like that. I'm a lone parent so sometimes I had to drag my kids with me. It was hard, I had to choose my fights.

Later, I was a nursery nurse. My son was starting university and he said: 'Mum, why don't you start university. Why don't you go and do politics?' Within a week I'd handed my notice in. I did a Politics and Sociology degree and while I was there I worked part-time in Asda.

I didn't even know there was a union in Asda, and one day there was someone in, recruiting. He asked me if I wanted to join, and I did, and the next time he was in, he asked me if I wanted to be a rep. My sister was dying at that time, so I couldn't do it. But he was in again a few years later and I'd had a few run-ins with managers and heard about bad things happening to colleagues, so I said: 'I'll be a rep.'

The Asda distribution centres are a male-dominated area of the business. They get more pay than those of us working in the stores, but their jobs aren't any more important or significant than ours. For instance, I work in the George clothing department. They are loading up deliveries for dispatch to the stores, and then I'm taking delivery of them. I do everything they do, only in reverse. Yet they get paid more. It clearly is discrimination and it pisses me off. I've got two granddaughters who are 12 and 14, and I think: 'God, this is still going on.' I don't like it. I'm angry.

I wouldn't have known if it wasn't for people in the union telling me. That's what a union can do – find out the facts and highlight them for the workforce, and then mobilise people. I have to say, though, a lot of people didn't sign up for the union and the Equal Pay campaign because they were frightened they'd lose their jobs.

The union organised meetings in the local town hall. I went to those and spoke with them. They told me we had a strong legal case – there were no promises, but they seemed really sure, or they wouldn't have put so much money and effort into the case.

We began doing demonstrations outside Asda shops. Then Asda changed our contracts and we went down to their headquarters in Leeds and combined it with the Equal Pay protests. They tried to get us removed from outside the HQ. But we have had wins in court now, about equal value and equal jobs. Colleagues of mine have had to go back down to Leeds and swear under oath about their jobs to prove what they do.

It has gone on for a long time – they are good at dragging out the legal side of it. Some staff think it'll never happen – that we'll never get equal pay. It has been so long and they've given up. They worry, and they whisper about equal pay in the canteen and I ask why they're whispering. It's because they're worried a manager can hear them. I say 'So what?! It's going nothing to do with him. It's to do with Walmart.' Managers have undermined our willpower, chipped away at it, whispered into the young ones' ears: 'Don't join the union', things like that. And I can't wait to get equal pay so I can go and see them...

I've no doubt we'll win. It's sad because we've seen colleagues die without an end result – we lost one to Covid, for instance. And I'm sad she'll not get to see us win the victory.

Carers during Covid

Shona Thomson

While an enhanced reablement homecare worker in Glasgow, Shona became a union rep. In 2017, she became a branch secretary, and in 2019 a full-time GMB convenor. Then Covid infested the country and care workers were put at profound risk. Here she details the struggles that followed, and how union members responded.

THE FEAR WHEN Covid started was huge. I had women who had been doing the job for years crying because they were so frightened for themselves. It takes a certain type of person to be a home carer. Visiting complete strangers' homes initially can be daunting. It's a demanding role. These women love doing this job – or they did love doing this job. When Covid hit further barriers and struggles emerged. The country went into a panic but so did the governments and employers. Care workers suddenly became numbers. This has shown the lack of duty of care directed towards care workers themselves. Their physical and mental health suffered greatly.

Our first challenge was the PPE issue. That was something as a union we had to press for. These women had to feel safer to alleviate their fears and stresses. So GMB had to campaign for PPE to be adequate to protect against Covid – not just your usual plastic apron and gloves, that was always worn pre-Covid. The only additional things we could get at that point were masks. How was this fair? Covid was there, highly transmissible regardless of whether in a clinical setting or not. Type 2 FRSM were initially awarded to the carers and then taken away. So, within the GMB union we had an instant health and safety issue. Right away a campaign started – GMB wrote an open letter with thousands of signatures to the Scottish Government. It worked, additional PPE entitlement changed and Type 2 fluid-resistant surgical masks were reinstated.

Then an issues arose regarding our care workers who should have been shielding, according to government guidelines, but weren't permitted to because they didn't have a government letter. Even though they were vulnerable – asthmatic, COPD etc – the employer was denying them the right to shield. GMB fought these battles and won; we made sure our members were reassured. After that, all our workers who should have been shielding were.

The home carers at this point only had two tunic uniforms. This meant home carers who were working a split shift would be out in the workplace wearing contaminated uniforms as they were dealing with people who were Covid positive and then having to go from one service user to the next, without adequate PPE coverage.

Carers also felt great fear when they arrived at their own front doors. It was a case of stripping off everything, putting it all into a plastic bag, and then into a washing machine without touching anything. Then they'd be straight into a shower. They were trying to protect their own homes and families from Covid whilst at the same time doing their jobs. The pressure was tremendous on all levels, both at work and at home, during the national lockdown from March to August 2020.

This led to carers on split shifts not going home during their split breaks, firstly to keep their families safe, and also to avoid having to continuously decontaminate themselves by showering and washing uniforms. There were no facilities available in-between shifts apart from if they went home. They had to sit in bus shelters and do things like that as nowhere else was open during national lockdown. We asked for mobile help – vans with hot drinks, for instance – but got nothing. The lack of support in that first lockdown for home carers was shocking. The unforeseen pressures they worked under to protect our vulnerable society was immense, and had such an impact on their physical and mental wellbeing at that point. I'm crying now thinking about it, remembering the fear, stress and anxiety of each call from our workforce.

We had a big battle requesting more overalls. They said the tunics would take too long to order so they were going to get polo shirts. A thousand or so arrived but very few home carers received these much-needed additional uniforms. Wherever they went, it wasn't to the majority of home carers working in the communities.

The employer's operational team didn't want to listen to what we and our sister union, Unison, were saying. They wouldn't listen to the experiences of the homeworkers. From day one, GMB asked for a Covid Response Team that could go in properly equipped where there was a positive case. This would have mitigated against virus transmission. They said this wasn't possible. You were hitting a brick wall with suggestions; they'd made their minds up.

By May and June 2020, we had got PPE – so that was a victory – and got it out to the carers. Then we had to challenge to get face visors. We had carers out there dealing with bodily fluids four times a day. If that person was positive, then they were at risk. There were things that could've been done as I've said previously but again, they weren't interested in what the workers were saying. Government guidelines had to be followed.

In the summer of 2020, when the first lockdown was lifted, there were still issues. There were issues around our shielders coming back to work. On August 1st, when that was due to happen, the Scottish Government hadn't yet provided an Occupational Health Risk Assessment. So, the employer's Operations Department phoned around shielding carers in the two weeks up to 1st August. The desperation to get carers back resulted in vulnerable carers being coerced back to work when they shouldn't have returned at that point. And when we wanted to stop those particular carers being put into the homes of Covid positive service users, we were told: 'No, they've got their PPE on, they'll be fine'. There was no understanding that these carers had been shielded for that mitigating reason, to avoid Covid. Nor about the physical or mental health impact the person endured. All they looked at was numbers to cover the service. Again, that duty of care was never there for the home carers themselves. Although the Corporate Employer department had these mitigations in place, Operations on some levels chose to differ.

When Covid testing came in, residential carers were getting regular PCR testing. Home carers were only tested if they were symptomatic. They'd then have to go through their manager, who would then 'Okay' them to go for a test. GMB felt they also should be entitled to a weekly home test – we did a consultative ballot with members which came back over 90 per cent in agreement. So, we got that concession but only because we were about to go to industrial action. That started in January 2021 after ten months without any mitigations in place apart from a plastic apron and gloves and a mask and visor.

At the start of the pandemic, in terms of reps, there was me, a part-time member of staff and another rep being trained. But since then, I've managed to recruit another eight home care reps and get them trained. They were very keen to become reps. They know their workplace colleagues need support, and recognise inequality.

When workplace issues and the need to challenge employers arise, the protection, support and security your union gives is that you're not just a number, you're a person, you're important and you matter.

From Timex to Better Than Zero

Stella Rooney

Dundee's 1993 Timex dispute was a seminal moment in Scottish history. Bringing together her role as an artist and her union activism, in her work Stella has told the story of Timex and shown how yesterday's industrial world relates to issues faced by young workers today.

I'M 23 NOW and when I was 17 I joined the STUC's Better Than Zero campaign, just as it was getting set up. We did a lot of flash mobs and campaigning outside different hospitality and retail venues in Glasgow. That led to involvement with trade unions, and meeting other young people working in precarious workplace like me. I was working in a café where pay was low and there was a lot of bullying. So Better Than Zero was my introduction, and then I joined Unite and got involved in general campaigning. It was meeting with other young people with similar issues that lit my interest.

Better Than Zero created a space for young workers to articulate what they were facing. There are lots of issues that all workers share, but some that are specific to young workers – precarious work tends to affect younger workers more, and pay rates are different for younger people. I know so many people who got involved in the years after that and I think the work of that campaign gave a lot of young trade unionists confidence to go out and be active members wherever they've gone on to work. It has shifted the culture in Scotland.

I've always been interested in working class history, but when I was studying in Dundee I was really interested in the way de-industrialisation shapes the world that we live in. As a young woman who up to that point had only worked in hospitality, I was interested in this world of work where people had skills, and well-paid, unionised jobs. It didn't exist to me and my friends. That is the perspective I am interested in, though it's not to say that everything about that period of time was better. I don't want to look at it just with nostalgia, but I am really interested in the way that the world of work and the world that young people have inherited has changed.

I'm not interested in saying 'Oh this was great, we should do this again' but I think people my age don't always know how it used to be, and that informs your expectations of what we can achieve. So I'm interested in reflecting on that artistically, but also saying 'Well, why can't we have union recognition in a bar or a restaurant if they had it in a factory?' Because these are the factories of the world we live in now.

In my final year of art school, I decided that I wanted to make a film about the role of Timex in Dundee. I was interested in Timex because there were still so many people around who had lived through it. It had become a huge thing. I think it's really important to feature the factory workers' voices because they're not often heard – the ruling class aren't interested. As an artist who is a socialist I want to build working class power and support the trade union movement.

Timex was something really new to me, especially as a Glaswegian living in Dundee. Dundee has such interesting history anyway, from the jute industry through to technology. I was interested in the fact that many of the workers involved in the dispute were women and how Dundee at different points in its history has been described as a matriarchal city, because often women were working more than men. Sometimes that was about the perceived dexterity of women's fingers compared to men's, and they went to the jute factories, and later to Timex and other skilled places.

Timex is interesting because it was one of the last industrial fights. The fact it closed was not due to the lack of willpower or strength of the workforce, but down to us transitioning to a globalised economy where the labour could be outsourced more cheaply elsewhere. Timex was a really important part of Dundee's social fabric and culture, and when the factory closed it was a bitter moment for the city. People still talk about it now.

As a young trade unionist, there's a lot I find inspiring about the bravery and convictions of the workers there and also the way that up until the closure, the strength of trade unionism in that workplace meant that people had better wages and a higher quality of life. The factory was about more than just the final strike. Over the years, thousands of people worked there and it made a big mark on the city.

People have an idea of trade unions as a thing of the past or something just for men who work in factories. Although we know that's not true, I see my role as an artist as to trying to dispel some of that. Timex for example was not heavily male and many women worked in the factory. There is this real pride in these legacies of industry. People were proud of their work and still are. They look back fondly on the sense of community they had there, and as a young person growing up in a world which is quite different I think we can learn from creating that kind of community in a workplace and beyond.

I know lots of people who are organising in the hospitality sector right now and they are trying to create a culture of community and solidarity in the face of hostile employers. When you look back and see how people did that in industries of the past, you can make the link, and see how young trade unionists today are inheriting this past. We don't have to reinvent the wheel. While some things will be different because the nature of work has changed, there's lots we should be proud to continue in our trade union activism today.

Workers in the gig economy

Xabier Villares

Through his job as a delivery rider, Xabier saw the conditions that gig economy workers toil under. He helped found the Workers' Observatory Project, which seeks to challenge conditions in self-employed work and considers the future role of trade unions.

I HAVE WORKED as a rider full-time and part-time. You could earn more four years ago than you can now. At peak times the money can be OK, but you have to balance that with the lack of holiday pay and there are risks, like being between buses all day. There can be accidents. Many things are not covered, so you have to look after yourself.

The most difficult thing is not really knowing how things are working in the app. You are working with a computer, you don't have a manager. Your boss is an algorithm. You can email in with a question and you might get an answer, but most of the time you are alone in the street with your bike and the app. You don't know how the algorithms work and how it affects your income, and how it decides where you need to go and the time you have to spend on each order. Plus, they can terminate the contract whenever they want. It is very precarious. Tomorrow they can say: this is over because we have received a complaint and you cannot do a thing. You are out, and that is it.

They have no obligation to get you any work. You can be out there for six hours and you don't know what that day's income will be, never. There are peak times when it easier to get orders, but you don't know. Sometimes there are extra fees – incentives to go out. But they do this to have a massive number of people riding so at the same time they can charge lower prices for orders. So in the end, you are earning less. These extra fees are a trap.

Trade unions have started to understand better how things really work for us. But they are beginning a big shift towards understanding the changes in the world of work. Most of the unions are not prepared, but they are starting to change. They have started to speak to riders and organise.

The way workers organise themselves in the future is going to be different for many reasons. Precarious jobs are sometimes not someone's only job, but a job they do for extra income to pay rent and bills. And we are not in a factory or supermarket with all the workers around in the same place. We are spread around with the same problems, but with no places to talk about it. Perhaps the unions could provide these kind of spaces and build something on that. It is not easy, but they need to understand big data, algorithms, how this is changing work. That's for riders and other realms.

The Workers' Observatory Project started a couple of years ago. It was a gathering of researchers and gig economy workers. We began to talk about what our concerns were, especially about our incomes and how they were calculated. And we began to receive support from the STUC.

We realised we could articulate something together, something the unions could take part in too, so we tried to design something that wasn't to substitute unions, but to collaborate. It has been interesting to learn more and understand. And we have started to have international meetings with observatories in Italy, Spain, Belgium and elsewhere.

We see a big role for trade unions in all of this. Unions are always necessary. This is about workers changing the situation so we need to have enough strength to put our demands on the table. It is about renovation, new techniques and understanding big data and how it is changing everything. It is about the way we consume and produce. Unions must be there and must be smart to see that. So of course, there will be a role played by unions.

Acknowledgements

Deepest thanks to the STUC for offering me the opportunity to bring together this book – it has been a privilege. The encouragement of the STUC 125th Anniversary Project Advisory Group has been invaluable, as has the creativity and perseverance of Linda Somerville, and the commitment of Yusef Akgun. I have also received fantastic and inventive backing from Rozanne Foyer and Dave Moxham. Their colleagues at Scottish Union Learning, Tommy Breslin and Wendy Burton, also offered valued support.

This book looks great because of the wonderful art of Maria Stoian and the ever-excellent photography of Alan McCredie. In making the book into an object, Jennie Renton and her colleague Maddie Mankey have been magnificent, as have the Luath team of Gavin MacDougall, Eilidh MacLennan, Rachael Murray, Scott Kemp and colleagues.

Love and unending thanks to my own little team of Marisa, Kaitlyn and Homer the cat.

Most of all, though, this book exists because of every trade unionist that helped, whether by offering ideas and contacts, being interviewed or agreeing to be photographed. They have been a reinvigorating, inspiring presence over the last year.

About the STUC

The Scottish Trade Union Congress aims to build a strong, influential and globally aware trade union movement that champions equalities and delivers a fundamental shift in wealth, wellbeing and power towards workers, our families and communities in Scotland and beyond. Representing over 550,000 trade union members, the STUC supports trade unions to educate, agitate and organise to build a strong and diverse movement for change in our workplaces and communities.

Luath Press Limited

committed to publishing well written books worth reading

LUATH PRESS takes its name from Robert Burns, whose little collie Luath (*Gael.*, swift or nimble) tripped up Jean Armour at a wedding and gave him the chance to speak to the woman who was to be his wife and the abiding love of his life. Burns called one of the 'Twa Dogs' Luath after Cuchullin's hunting dog in Ossian's *Fingal*. Luath Press was established in 1981 in the heart of Burns country, and is now based a few steps up the road from Burns' first lodgings on Edinburgh's Royal Mile. Luath offers you distinctive writing with a hint of unexpected pleasures.

Most bookshops in the UK, the US, Canada, Australia, New Zealand and parts of Europe, either carry our books in stock or can order them for you. To order direct from us, please send a £sterling cheque, postal order, international money order or your credit card details (number, address of cardholder and expiry date) to us at the address below. Please add post and packing as follows: UK – £1.00 per delivery address; overseas surface mail – £2.50 per delivery address; overseas airmail – £3.50 for the first book to each delivery address, plus £1.00 for each additional book by airmail to the same address. If your order is a gift, we will happily enclose your card or message at no extra charge.

Luath Press Limited
543/2 Castlehill
The Royal Mile
Edinburgh EH1 2ND
Scotland
Telephone: +44 (0)131 225 4326 (24 hours)
Email: sales@luath.co.uk
Website: www.luath.co.uk